SINGLEFOCUS

GEORGE
BARNA

Regal

From Gospel Light
Ventura, California, U.S.A.

PUBLISHED BY REGAL BOOKS
FROM GOSPEL LIGHT
VENTURA, CALIFORNIA, U.S.A.
PRINTED IN THE U.S.A.

Regal Books is a ministry of Gospel Light, an evangelical Christian publisher dedicated to serving the local church. We believe God's vision for Gospel Light is to provide church leaders with biblical, user-friendly materials that will help them evangelize, disciple and minister to children, youth and families.

It is our prayer that this Regal book will help you discover biblical truth for your own life and help you meet the needs of others. May God richly bless you.

For a free catalog of resources from Regal Books/Gospel Light, please call your Christian supplier or contact us at 1-800-4-GOSPEL *or* www.regalbooks.com.

Revised edition. Originally published as *Single Adults* by Issachar Resources in 2002.

Cover and interior design by Robert Williams
Edited by Amy Simpson

Library of Congress Cataloging-in-Publication Data

Barna, George.
  Single focus / George Barna.
      p. cm.
Includes bibliographical references.
  ISBN 0-8307-2958-5
  1. Church work with single people. 2. Single people—Religious life.
I. Title.
  BV4437 .B37 2003
  259'.086'52—dc21   2002152024

1 2 3 4 5 6 7 8 9 10 11 12 13 14 15 / 09 08 07 06 05 04 03

Rights for publishing this book in other languages are contracted by Gospel Light Worldwide, the international nonprofit ministry of Gospel Light. Gospel Light Worldwide also provides publishing and technical assistance to international publishers dedicated to producing Sunday School and Vacation Bible School curricula and books in the languages of the world. For additional information, visit www.gospellightworldwide.org; write to Gospel Light Worldwide, P.O. Box 3875, Ventura, CA 93006; or send an e-mail to info@gospellightworldwide.org.

CONTENTS

1/19

106542

ACKNOWLEDGMENTS

Here's my confession. Even though I have written a book about single adults, I am married and have been for 24 years, which is a long time removed from living as a bachelor. I have never experienced a divorce—okay, on some days it seemed like a better alternative than staying married, but my wife and I resisted the impulse—and my parents never got divorced either, so I do not have any personal experience with being single through divorce. If the probabilities hold true, my wife will outlive me, so I won't know what widowerhood is like either. What this boils down to is that the only thing that qualifies me to write this book is the extensive research that my company, the Barna Research Group, and I have conducted among single adults on a wide range of topics. It is my fervent hope that single adults are able to tell you their story adequately and accurately through the research.

Not only can I not claim to have personal knowledge of what it's like to be single, but I cannot even take sole credit for the research about our subjects. I am blessed with a terrific team of professionals with whom I have the honor of working. You should know who you are. In alphabetical order (I feared there might be a backlash if I listed them chronologically) they are Rachel Ables, Irene Castillo, Jim Fernbaugh, Meg Flammang, Lynn Gravel, Cameron Hubiak, Pam Jacob, David Kinnaman, Carmen Moore, Julie Oxenreider, Dan Parcon, Celeste Rivera and Kim Wilson. This is my primary internal team. The Lord has blessed me with a great group of people—folks who love Jesus, who are committed to His work and who are capable professionals. I thank God for them, am grateful for their continued patience with my own faults and idiosyncrasies and am humbled that they remain passionate about the vision that God has entrusted to us in relation to His purposes. It is a joy to work with them and to see how God directs our efforts.

And then there is my external team. Included in that group are the pastors of my home churches—Larry DeWitt and Larry Osborne—who, along with the staffs and lay ministers, fortify us with their prayers and ministry. Developing resource materials for ministries has become an act of spiritual warfare, and it is the prayers and encouragement of these spiritual warriors that sustain us.

Sealy Yates, Curtis Yates and John Eames are also on the external team as my literary agents. How wonderful it is to have trustworthy and competent professionals who genuinely care about me, my ministry and their role in furthering that outreach.

And, of course, there is my personal team—my family. They are God's unique and special blessing to me. About two decades ago my wife, Nancy, helped me launch Barna Research and has guided it from day one to financial stability and operational nimbleness. She takes on greater responsibility during my frenetic writing periods, handling the increased load with great aplomb. My daughters Samantha and Corban have been endlessly loving, forgiving and enjoyable. With every book I write they sacrifice time that I should be spending with them, so that I may have the opportunity to communicate truths that (we hope) will bless and help people. They deserve magnificent blessings for all they do to enable books like this to emerge.

Finally, I must thank the Lord Himself for continuing to find a use for me in His kingdom. I would have been tired of my nonsense by now if I were He, but I suppose that's one of the zillion reasons why He is God and I am not. May this book honor and glorify Him and be useful in the pursuit of His purposes and in the development of His kingdom. What a privilege it is to know Him, to love Him and to serve Him.

GEORGE BARNA

C H A P T E R 1

YOU'RE NOT ALONE
IF YOU'RE SINGLE

Did you know that in four states you may legally get married at age 12?

If you guessed that the European nations often described as the sex capitals of the world, such as Denmark and Holland, have the highest divorce rates on Earth, you would be exactly . . . wrong. The United States holds that dubious distinction.

Were you aware that there are more widowed people in the U.S. than the entire populations of more than four dozen nations of the world, including Belgium, Bolivia, the Czech Republic, Denmark, Ecuador, Greece, Guatemala, Hungary, Ireland, Israel, New Zealand, Norway, Portugal and Sweden?[1]

Although many women complain about the lack of single men, did you know that there are 4 million more males who have never been married than there are never-been-married females?[2]

You may realize that more than 4 out of 5 Americans call themselves Christian and that the Christian faith discourages divorce. But have you heard that born-again adults have the same likelihood of seeing their marriage end in divorce as do non-Christians?[3]

Would you be surprised to learn that the United States has more single adults than any other nation in the world except China and India; or that the number of singles in the U.S. exceeds the total national population of all but 11 of the world's 192 nations?[4]

How shocked would you be to discover that the number of single parents in the United States is greater than the entire population of Colorado and Tennessee combined?[5]

As devastating as divorce is for most women, did you know that three-quarters of them get remarried?[6]

At the turn of the twentieth century, just 1 percent of all adults were divorced. Were you aware that the figure has grown tenfold since then?[7]

Do you know what they call the most attractive men in singles bars? Married. (Sorry, just wanted to see if you were paying attention.)

Whether you examine their lifestyles, demographics or religious beliefs and practices, the growing population of single adults in America is full of surprises. Understanding the character of unmarried Americans is important, not just for the sake of knowledge, but in order to minister effectively to them and alongside them.

SHIFTING VALUES

Old impressions die hard. Many Americans—older Americans, in particular—assume that people cannot be happy and fulfilled unless they find a marriage partner or a soul mate. In the past quarter century, however, things have changed dramatically. Our perspectives on commitment and loyalty have changed. Methods of communication and desirable vocational skills have shifted. Personal relationships develop differently from the past, and sexual relations apart from marriage have become common. Cohabitation, divorce and parenting by grandparents have skyrocketed. Tolerance of different, nontraditional lifestyles has increased. More than ever before, Americans seek the benefits of intimate relationships without the pressures and perceived limitations of marriage. That helps to explain why people wait longer and experiment more broadly and creatively with a spectrum of relationships and lifestyles prior to marriage.

> MORE THAN EVER BEFORE, AMERICANS SEEK THE BENEFITS OF INTIMATE RELATIONSHIPS WITHOUT THE PRESSURES AND PERCEIVED LIMITATIONS OF MARRIAGE.

It is common for novels, television programs, contemporary music, movies and videos to sanction nontraditional values and family arrangements. This media influence can be seen in the transformation of the nation's thinking and behavior. The black and Hispanic populations of the U.S. are often the early—and most prolific—adopters of these new living configurations, but the record shows that the white and Asian populations waste little time in jumping onto the bandwagon.

TABLE 1.1

THE SHIFT FROM MARRIAGE TO SINGLEHOOD

	All Adults 18+			Whites			Blacks			Hispanics		
	1980	1990	1999	1980	1990	1999	1980	1990	1999	1980	1990	1999
MAR	66%	62%	60%	67%	64%	62%	51%	46%	41%	66%	62%	59%
NBM	20	22	24	19	20	21	31	35	39	24	27	29
DIV	6	8	10	6	8	10	8	11	12	6	7	8
WID	8	8	7	8	8	7	10	9	8	4	4	4

Key: MAR=married; NBM=never-been-married; DIV=divorced; WID=widowed.
Source: U.S. Bureau of the Census, *Statistical Abstract of the United States*, 2000 (Washington, DC), table 53.

Differentiating Singles Groups

If we limit our discussion of single adults to those who have never been married or have experienced divorce, we will overlook important segments of the singles population. With advances in health care and medicine, people are living longer than ever before, leading to the precipice of an explosion in the number of widowed adults living in the U.S. These individuals typically represent the two oldest generations in the nation, the Seniors and the Builders—two groups whose moral foundations differ considerably from those of younger citizens. Adults 55 and older experience a comparatively low divorce rate, but they face a high probability of living a significant number of their twilight years as singles.

And how can we neglect single parents, a subset within the singles niches already described? In many cases, these adults had children while married, yet those who had children out of wedlock have become the

> TO THINK THAT ALL SINGLE ADULTS ARE ALIKE, AND THUS TO RELATE TO THEM IN AN IDENTICAL MANNER, IS A GRIEVOUS MISTAKE.

fastest-growing category of single parents. The enlightenment brought on by a seemingly endless gush of articles and special reports on the plight of children and mothers of broken marriages has had little apparent impact on curtailing the growth of this household type.

Those who are legally married but physically separated from their spouse comprise the final singles niche to consider. This group—sometimes referred to as "the divorced-in-waiting"—is the smallest of the singles subpopulations. For many separated individuals, this state of marital ambiguity is "hell on Earth." It is a state of confusion and uncertainty that usually solves few, if any, of their marital problems, but raises a plethora of gut-wrenching questions and challenges. The results of separation are relatively predictable. On average, 97 percent of white women who separate from their husband are divorced within five years of the separation. (Though not as universal, the same outcome occurs for three-quarters of nonwhite women who undergo a separation.)[8]

In summary, America has five distinct singles groups: the never-been-married, the divorced, the widowed, single parents and the separated. To think that all single adults are alike, and thus to relate to them in an identical manner, is a grievous mistake. But it is one often made as we lump unmarried people into a single, massive population.

THE LIFE CYCLE

Some measure of our family status can be attributed to age and life situations—what is commonly known as the life cycle. Some of the choices we make are dictated by cultural pressures, such as the expectation of getting married while a 20-something. Other decisions are determined by age and physiological parameters such as women having babies during those years when they are physically capable of producing them (i.e., teen years through the mid-40s). Overall, many of the decisions we make are an outgrowth of these life-cycle phenomena.

Marital status is also affected by the life cycle. People tend to get married (for the first time, at least) during their 20s, as they settle into a career, a geographic location and a universe of personal and organizational relationships. Eager to experience the challenges and joys of parenthood, most couples begin having children between their mid-20s and mid-30s. Economic and professional pressures, the development of divergent interests and a variety of sexual tensions often lead to divorce, commonly occurring between a person's mid-30s and mid-40s. Remarriage usually occurs within a few years of the initial divorce. After a period of settling down, which frequently occurs during a person's 40s, 50s or 60s, the final phase of most people's life cycle unfolds upon reaching their mid-60s or early 70s. Occupational retirement, physical limitations and widowhood often define this final life stage.

Statistics bear out these patterns. Among people 18 to 24, nearly 9 out of 10 (87 percent) have never been married. That figure drops to just one-quarter (24 percent) among those who are in the 25 to 44 age bracket. In the 35 to 54 age group, however, divorce becomes more prevalent. More than one-third of the adults in this segment have gone through at least one divorce, and two-thirds of them have remarried. The incidence of widowhood jumps once people reach 65, rising from fewer than 1 in 10 among people 55 to 64 years old (and, of course, much lower percentages among younger adults) to a whopping one-third of those who reach the traditional retirement age.[9]

The data in table 1.2 portrays a fairly predictable course of change and challenge. As people age, new opportunities, risks and dangers await us in each life phase. For most people, the early years of adulthood pose the fundamental marital challenge—whether or not to get married, with whom and when. After a person gets married, within the first decade of the relationship the partners are confronted by pressures that may potentially dissolve that union. Then, for most people who get divorced, a return to the premarital phase of trying to determine whether or not to get married (again), with whom and when occurs. The final chapter of the tale typically begins when people enter the mid-60s, at which time they begin to harbor concerns about the potential death of their marriage partner.

TABLE 1.2

THE MARRIAGE LIFE CYCLE

Age	NBM	DIV	WID	SEP	MAR
18-24	87%	1%	*	1%	13%
25-34	34	7	*	3	53
35-44	16	13	1	3	64
45-54	8	15	3	3	70
55-64	5	14	9	2	72
65+	3	5	31	1	55

Key: NBM=never-been-married; DIV=divorced; WID=widowed; SEP=separated; MAR=married.
* Indicates less than half of 1 percent.
Source: U.S. Bureau of the Census, "Table A1: Marital Status of People 15 Years and Over, by Age, Sex, Personal Earnings, Race and Hispanic Origin/March 2000," Census Bureau Home Page, released June 29, 2001. http://www.census.gov/ (accessed June 29, 2001).

NEVER BEEN DOWN THE AISLE

In the past, there was a social stigma associated with reaching your 20s and not being married. Today, however, the median age of a first marriage has risen to 25 among women and 27 among men. Unmarried young people used to face a barrage of questions such as, What's taking you so long? Why aren't you married yet? Young singles used to fear the stream of behind-the-back whispers saying that there must be something wrong with a person who wasn't wed by their mid-20s. Today, though, the magnifying glass is placed over the choice by young people to get married. Now they are the ones peppered with such questions as, What's your hurry? Why are you getting married? Why not just live with the person?

The Census Bureau informs us that among people 15 and older, the never-been-married segment is now 60 million strong—32 million men and 28 million women.[10] About one-third of that population, however, is 20 or younger. If we limit the inquiry to people 18 and older, we're speaking about a population of 48 million, of which nearly half is under 25. One-quarter of the never-been-married group is 25 to 34 years old, while the remaining one-quarter is 35 or older. As evidence of the widespread draw of marriage in our land, only 4 percent of all people 55 or older have never ventured into a marriage. In spite of the sweeping changes that are altering our lifestyles and values, an undeniable fact remains: Few Americans die without having taken a dip in the marriage pond.

However, even within the never-been-married public, there are distinct demographic patterns. For instance, while two-thirds of all white adults in the 25 to 34 age segment have been married, fewer than half of the black adults in the same age group have experienced marriage. Racial identification enters the picture in a big way. Since 1980, there has been an approximate 11 percent increase in the white never-been-married contingent. However, that pales in comparison to the growth within the black (26 percent) and Hispanic (21 percent) populations. Among blacks, this growth is driven by a determination to experience having a family without getting married, while the Hispanics have a profusion of young people waiting until later ages to get married.

TABLE 1.3

THE PREVALENCE OF STABLE MARRIAGES HAS DROPPED IN THE PAST HALF CENTURY

Year	NBM	DIV	WID	MAR
2000	28%	9%	6%	56%
1990	26	8	7	59
1980	26	6	7	61
1970	25	3	8	64
1960	22	2	8	68
1950	23	2	8	67

Key: NBM=never-been-married; DIV=divorced; WID=widowed; MAR=married.
Source: U.S. Bureau of the Census, "Table MS-1: Current Population Reports Series P20-514," *Census Bureau Home Page,* 2001. http://www.census.gov/ (accessed 2001).

SHATTERED DREAMS

As millions of Americans will attest, getting married and staying married are two entirely different matters. The sad reality is that roughly half of all marriages end in divorce within 15 years of the wedding day.[11] At any given time, about 1 out of 10 adults are currently divorced. However, the percentage of adults who have been married and divorced is much higher, because a majority of those who get divorced eventually remarry. Overall, one-third of the adult population that has been married has also been through at least one divorce.[12] Among people in the 30 to 49 age bracket, that figure is close to half.

The average age of a person at the time of their first marriage is 26; the average age of a married person's first divorce is 34. In fact, age is firmly correlated with divorce: The younger a woman is when she gets married, the more likely her marriage will result in divorce. Six out of 10 marriages among women who get married before their eighteenth birthday wind up in divorce, compared with just one-third among women who marry after their twentieth birthday.

It seems inevitable that in America's immediate future its citizens will be increasingly comfortable with, accepting of and even expectant of marriages fizzling in divorce. Some researchers have posited that we have shifted out of an evolutionary period regarding divorce (when we questioned our fundamental ideas about marriage, parenting, moral values and relationships) into a revolutionary period (in which we accept divorce and other nontraditional relationships as emotionally and spiritually viable, legally valid and morally reasonable).[13] The fact remains that almost nobody enters a marriage seeking to divorce, but more and more we find that the people who go through a divorce are emotionally and morally resigned to the fact that it is a normal, if not inevitable, life experience.

REDEFINED FAMILIES

A century ago, relatively few single parents existed, and most of those people fell into that state because of the premature death of a spouse. Birth out of wedlock, divorce and cohabitation were social taboos yet to gain widespread acceptance. In 1900, fewer than 1 out of every 100 adults was a single parent of a child under 18. Today, there are more than 12 million single parents with children under 18 in their care—about 6 percent of all adults, and roughly 1 out of every 3 families.[14] That total has tripled since 1970. In fact, 28 percent of the nation's children presently live with just one of their birth parents. The implication of the growth of single-parent households is that a majority of the children born this year are likely to live in a single-parent home for some period of time prior to celebrating their eighteenth birthday.

The world of single parenthood is changing. More than 4 out of 5 single parents (84 percent) are mothers. However, two significant trends are altering that reality. The first is the steady increase in single fathers being given custody of their children. Between 1990 and 2000, the number of single fathers with primary custody of children under the age of 18 leaped by 62 percent, while the growth among single moms expanded by 25 percent. Once thought to be detrimental to the needs of the children, recent research shows just the opposite regarding fathers filling the role of the primary postdivorce parent. Because custodial fathers tend to be older, better educated, better paid and more highly motivated to care for their children, as well as resolved to involve the mother, a growing number of cases show single fathers doing a commendable job of providing their kids with a viable home environment.

The second pattern worth noting is that a growing proportion of single parents are not divorced but had their children without marrying the other birth parent. Among women who are single moms, 40 percent were never married to the father of their children. Among men who are single-parents, 35 percent were not wedded to the mother of their children. Given the continued growth in births outside of marriage, and the psychological acceptance of this practice our nation has embraced, we can also expect continued growth in the number of single parents who have never been married.

THE PREMATURELY DEPARTED

Losing a spouse through death is not something a person has much reason to anticipate—until they reach their 60s. While there are tragic stories of young marrieds who suffer the premature loss of a spouse, those stories are exceptions. Fewer than two-tenths of 1 percent of all people under age 35 have been widowed, and fewer than 2 percent of adults in the 35 to 54 age group are widowed. Widowhood starts to become more of a possibility between the mid-50s and mid-60s, when about 9 percent lose their spouse to death. But once the 65-year-old threshold is reached, it becomes an ever-growing probability—17 percent of adults who are 65 to 69, 26 percent of those 70 to 74 and 46 percent of people 75 or older are widowed.[15]

Widowhood is an incredibly sexist experience—4 out of 5 adults who are single due to the death of their spouse are females. Whether this is attributable to the different priorities that men and women often embrace in life—men often develop their identity and sense of value on the basis of what they do, women on the basis of whom they love and connect with emotionally—or if it is attributable to other causes, the fact remains that widowhood is a much more likely experience for women than men.

Because the average life span of men and women differs by only two years, we are sometimes lured into thinking that the proportion of widowed individuals is likely to be similar as well. However, nearly half of all women 65 or older are widowed (45 percent), compared to just one-seventh of all men 65 or older (14 percent).[16] This becomes a shattering transition time for most widowers, entailing a massive change in lifestyle (e.g., 70 percent of all widowed adults live alone).

SHARED DEMOGRAPHICS

If we were to make the mistake of assuming that all single adults are the same, we would be accurate in assigning certain assessments to unmarried people. For instance, income levels are lower for all of the single-adult segments than for the married-couple population. Single adults are considerably less likely to own the home they live in (only about half do) than are married couples (4 out of 5 do).[17]And each of the single-adult segments has a lower level of educational achievement than do married couples.

However, there are significant differences regarding virtually every other demographic factor studied, and understanding the variance across the singles subgroups is crucial toward possessing a healthy and realistic view of singles.

Income levels are a good example. It is true that all single-adult segments have lower average incomes than do married couples, but the actual median levels for each group vary tremendously. At the low end of the spectrum are single women who have never been married; their median income level is barely above the poverty level in America! Single fathers, on the other hand, have the highest income level, close to $40,000 annually, which is still a far cry from the $54,276 registered among married couples, although distant from the edge of poverty. Single mothers live much closer to the edge of poverty, earning an average of a bit less than $25,000 annually, suggesting that along with emotional pressure, there is a great deal of financial pressure they must combat from day to day.[18]

Income disparities also arise among different racial and ethnic groups. The average black married couple has a median income of nearly $50,000, which is four times what black single women make and three times what black single mothers—who constitute the majority of all black mothers—earn each year. In the Hispanic community, married couples average only about $35,000 annually, resulting in a smaller financial gap between Hispanics who are married and those who are not. Of course, the same general pattern holds true for Hispanics: Single adults make substantially less (median of $16,805 among all singles) than their married-couple counterparts.[19]

WHAT TO LOOK FOR

As we work through our research on single adults, keep in mind that this is not a static population; social and personal changes will continue to redefine not only the number of single adults but also the nature of this population. Demographically, you may expect to see the following changes:

- In the next 30 years, the United States will experience a doubling of the population aged 65 or older. Thus, it is almost certain that the number of widows will dramatically increase.
- As immigration continues to increase the nation's population, as nonwhite segments grow at a faster rate than the white

population, as the proclivity of the nonwhite groups to have children out of wedlock remains, and as divorce rapidly grows among blacks and widowhood among Hispanics—all of these factors will inevitably reshape the singles population and its needs. Expect to hear more leaders demanding programs and services offered in different languages and using different strategic approaches to remain relevant to these growing niches.

• Various religious groups, scholars and public officials have raised awareness and public concern regarding the harsh realities of children being raised in a single-parent home by highlighting the underlying values that lead to nontraditional family units (e.g., low commitment, low loyalty, impermanence, unpredictability and emotional discontinuity). However, the evidence indicates that people usually do what has been modeled for them. Consequently, we may anticipate continued growth and acceptance of cohabitation, births outside of marriage and divorce among young people, especially within the black and Hispanic segments of society.

• The Hispanic and Asian populations in America are quite young. As those who are second- and third-generation immigrants of Asian and Latino heritage reach adulthood, and as a growing percentage of them enter the retirement years, the process of acculturation will further increase rates of divorce and widowhood.

FINAL THOUGHTS

Perhaps you're one of the many whose eyes glaze over at demographic statistics. *That's just numbers,* you may be thinking. *What about what's going on inside of these people? They're human beings. Marriage, divorce, widowhood— these are important mind-sets and experiences that give life to these people. The numbers are merely factoids unless they can help me learn how to love, serve and involve these people through meaningful activity. Help me get inside their heads and hearts rather than just their birth certificates and census data.*

I like demographic information—believe it or not—for it speaks to me in revealing ways. However, you're absolutely right to think that there is more, much more, to the lives of unmarried people than their demographic profile. And that's precisely what we will spend the rest of this book exploring—the self-perceptions, lifestyles, values, morals and spiritual realities of single adults. We'll get a sense of who single adults really are and how the three primary singles populations (i.e., never-been-married, divorced and widowed adults) differ from and mirror each other. Much of the information will come from surveys that my company, the Barna Research Group, has conducted over the past two years, which entail personal interviews covering a wide variety of topics among nearly 4,000 single adults randomly selected from across the nation. (To provide a point of comparison, I'll often allude to the interviews of more than 4,000 married adults we also conducted.)

Let's start the process of understanding single adults more deeply by exploring how they describe themselves.

THE SELF-IDENTIFICATION OF SINGLES

Much of what you do and don't do in life flows from your perception of yourself. Our self-view is founded upon a complex and ever-changing mixture of ideas concerning our psychological composure, our emotional makeup, our economic standing, our core behavioral choices, our values and our relationship with God. Those perceptions can either free us to pursue our dreams or shackle us to a prison of self-imposed limitations. Often, people juggle a mixture of freeing and limiting self-views.

One of the most surprising outcomes from our research is the tremendous similarity of self-perceptions between single and married adults. People categorize themselves in terms of their nationality, vocation, generation, faith affiliation, racial or ethnic orientation, sexual preference, affluence, ideological leanings and many other factors. Marital status is just one of several perspectives we consider when developing our self-view.

Similar or dissimilar, though, to live, serve and work in harmony with single adults demands a solid comprehension of their understanding of self.

PSYCHOLOGICAL AND EMOTIONAL SELF-PERCEPTIONS

One of the most significant elements of our self-view pertains to our assessment of how we relate to people. Overall, we found that single adults view themselves as highly relational; they like to have control without instigating conflict, and they are more likely to feel lonely or disconnected than are married individuals. They were notably more likely than married adults to eschew conflict, feel misunderstood by others and seek a handful of reliable friendships.

To get an accurate feel for these distinctions, we have to dissect the singles population into its component groups, for there are some important dissimilarities on these matters. For instance, singles who have never been married are more likely than any other adults, married or not, to be searching for a few good friends. About half of all never-been-marrieds are striving to develop additional relationships, which is considerably more common than the one-third of married adults who are also seeking to expand their extramarital relational ties. Presumably, one's spouse fills a substantial portion of one's relational needs. Divorced and widowed adults, while slightly more likely to be searching for meaningful relationships than married adults, are also older and more established in their lifestyles and, therefore, may feel more deeply connected than their younger, never-been-married counterparts. In the interest of bonding with others, it appears that never-been-marrieds may minimize their involvement in conflict.

The fact that the relational self-perceptions of divorced and widowed adults more closely reflect those of the married contingent may also suggest that age and life experience are more important than marital status in determining relationship capacity.

However, the fact that never-been-marrieds are almost twice as likely to feel that they are often misunderstood by others, and that even the divorced and widowed are almost 50 percent more likely to feel that way than married adults, suggests that the intimacy enjoyed through marriage goes a long way toward helping people feel that they get a fair hearing.

TABLE 2.1

SINGLES AND THEIR RELATIONSHIPS

Self-Description	SGL	NBM	WID	DIV	MAR
Avoid conflict whenever possible	76%	77%	81%	65%	65%
Like to be in control	68	70	60	72	64
Very relational	65	69	55	65	67
Trying to find a few good friends	47	52	40	41	34
Often misunderstood by others	43	46	38	37	27

Key: SGL=all single adults; NBM=never-been-married; WID=widowed; DIV=divorced; MAR=married.
Source: A national survey by the Barna Research Group, January 2000. The study randomly surveyed 1,002 adults, which included 469 single adults.

The data in table 2.1 point out that divorced people are slightly more likely than people from any other segment to enjoy control. Could this need for control have contributed to the split-up of their marriage? Also notice that the widowed niche occupied one end of the continuum when it came to conflict (they're more likely to avoid it), control (they're less anxious to have it) and being very relational (they're less likely to interact socially). In other words, widowed adults, who are generally in their mid-60s and beyond, want to "go along and get along." They may perceive their future to be too short to squander it by pursuing and battling with others.

More than 9 out of every 10 Americans, regardless of their marital state, think of themselves as self-sufficient. Most of us admit to being skeptical, too, although divorced adults lead the way in this regard. You can imagine that having endured the dissolution of a critical relationship with someone they trusted and in whom they had invested in knowing, they are now less prone to accept claims made by people whom they don't know as well.

TABLE 2.2

THE EMOTIONAL STATE OF ADULTS

Self-Description	SGL	NBM	WID	DIV	MAR
Self-sufficient	94%	92%	98%	95%	91%
Skeptical	61	58	53	71	56
Stressed-out	35	37	27	33	29

Key: SGL=all single adults; NBM=never-been-married; WID=widowed; DIV=divorced; MAR=married.
Source: A national survey by the Barna Research Group, January 2000. The study randomly surveyed 1,002 adults, which included 469 single adults.

Oddly, the highest stress level is exhibited by never-been-married adults: 4 out of 10 describe themselves as stressed-out (see table 2.2). Interviews revealed that such stress is generated by either their relational activities, their financial and career challenges, or both. Slightly fewer divorced individuals feel stressed-out (one-third), while even fewer widowed and married people admit such an emotional state (one-quarter).

ECONOMIC SELF-VIEW

A fairly clear and strong correlation exists between financial security and one's marital status. In table 2.3, notice that married people are substantially more likely than singles of any type to state that they are financially comfortable and less willing to suggest that they are struggling financially. It seems that divorce takes a deep toll on one's financial stability. Divorced adults were the only segment among whom less than half said they were financially comfortable. While a substantial portion of marriages dissolve at least in part due to financial tensions, the act of dismembering the marriage does not appear to alleviate the monetary difficulties that the partners experience. For millions of people, divorce heightens their financial tensions.

The issue of personal debt is intriguing as well. Nearly half of divorced adults and about 4 out of 10 married and never-been-married adults admit to being in debt. The widowed niche is least likely to adopt this self-view, with just 1 out of 5 embracing the label. But the types of debt differ for each group. Never-been-married adults face the costs of getting started in life: paying off college loans and car loans and acquiring the needs of basic living (e.g., furniture, clothing suitable for work and so on). Divorced adults struggle with debts incurred while married, such as alimony payments and the costs associated with starting over again. Widowed adults feel the least pinched because they are most likely to have their mortgages paid off, to have retirement and insurance benefits kicking in and to have learned how to keep their spending under control. (The U.S. Bureau of Labor also informs us that a greater percentage of older people than ever before are remaining in the work force, usually in part-time positions, but nevertheless are generating a small flow of revenue.) Many senior citizens also note that they have been preparing themselves for a change in lifestyle by downgrading their spending in order to match their reduced income after they retire.

TABLE 2.3

MONEY AND MARITAL STANDING

Self-Description	SGL	NBM	WID	DIV	MAR
Financially comfortable	56%	60%	63%	47%	70%
Personally struggling with finances	37	37	36	37	28
In debt	37	39	18	44	36

Key: SGL=all single adults; NBM=never-been-married; WID=widowed; DIV=divorced; MAR=married.
Source: A national survey by the Barna Research Group, January 2001. The study randomly surveyed 1,005 adults, which included 504 single adults.

Perhaps the most important outgrowth of this research, however, is the insight that among never-been-married and divorced adults, finances feel like the veritable sword of Damocles hung above their heads only by a single thread, ready to fall upon them at any moment. To maintain a desired standard of living, most couples feel they have no alternative but to have both partners bring in revenue. Therefore, it is not by accident that most married women, whether they have children or not, are employed. One of the dangers this raises, of course, is converting marriage into an economically driven arrangement rather than a permanent bond based upon shared love, experience and vision.

TIME AND ENERGY FOCUSED

Americans are world renowned for their frenetic pace of life, and most of us feel we can handle it. With one notable exception, only about half of all adults feel their lives are too busy: that exception is the widowed population, among whom just one-quarter suggest that they are too busy.

Views on the centrality of one's career vary widely when based on life stage and marital status, according to table 2.4. Never-been-marrieds, who are typically in their 20s or 30s, are by far the most likely to be career focused; nearly half say they fit the description of "career comes first in my life." In comparison, only 1 out of every 10 married adults make the same claim. Distracted by a plethora of other duties—mostly related to their marriage and children—married people are more likely to see their career as a means to an end, whereas never-been-marrieds tend to view their job (along with their personal relationships) as a defining reality. Divorced adults are caught in between these two views, with one-quarter admitting that their career is central in their life. Ample anecdotal evidence exists to support the notion that many marriages have failed because of the centrality of work for one or both spouses.

While our research did not dig deeply into the issue of addictions, a surprisingly large number of people admitted to struggling with an addiction of some type. Such obsessions were most common among those who have never wed and those who are divorced. The fact that 1 out of 5 divorced adults cited an addiction in their life may again point to a key reason why their marriage broke up or, in some cases, how they responded to the collapse of their marriage.

TABLE 2.4

DEFINED BY ACTIVITY

Self-Description	SGL	NBM	WID	DIV	MAR
Too busy	44%	47%	24%	53%	49%
Career comes first	32	43	14	27	11
Dealing with an addiction	13	13	5	18	8

Key: SGL=all single adults; NBM=never-been-married; WID=widowed; DIV=divorced; MAR=married.
Source: A series of nationwide surveys by the Barna Research Group, January 2000-November 2001. The study randomly surveyed 6,038 adults, which included 2,847 single adults.

TABLE 2.5

PREFERENCES THAT SHOW HOW WE VIEW OURSELVES

Self-Description	SGL	NBM	WID	DIV	MAR
Like to try new experiences	79%	88%	59%	75%	76%
Enjoy deep discussions	76	76	82	72	73
Like to keep things light	74	71	80	74	72
Concerned about the future	70	71	60	71	68
Concerned about the moral condition of the U.S.	70	64	83	74	79
Enjoy making tough decisions	52	53	49	50	52
Searching for meaning and purpose	51	55	44	44	35
Sociopolitical ideology:					
Mostly conservative	23	19	33	24	37
Mostly liberal	17	20	12	15	12

Key: SGL=all single adults; NBM=never-been-married; WID=widowed; DIV=divorced; MAR=married.
Source: A national survey by the Barna Research Group, January 2000. The study randomly surveyed 1,002 adults, which included 469 single adults.

The attitudinal preferences listed in table 2.5 illustrate how similar married and unmarried people are on many core perspectives—with the exception of widowed adults. Most people desire new experiences, especially among never-been-marrieds (essentially a generational thing) and least of all among the widowed. Nearly three-quarters of all adults also appreciate occasional deep discussions—even more so among widowed persons. Infrequent heavy conversation enables them to maintain both their hectic pace of life and their ability to remain optimistic and hopeful. However, adults generally like to keep things light.

Although, a study we conducted a few years ago showed that most adults are optimistic about the future and their place in it, 7 out of 10 singles regularly spend time pondering their future. Widowed adults are somewhat less likely to do so, but even a majority of our widowed citizens often consider the long-term possibilities that lie before them. In addition, most adults also spend time fretting over the moral state of the nation. This issue is less frequently and less seriously considered by never-been-married people compared with the other four niches we're exploring, but this also appears to be a function of both life cycle and generation.

About half of all adults say they enjoy making tough decisions. A similar portion of adults indicate that they are actively seeking an understanding of the meaning and purpose of life. For a matter that is fundamental toward guiding daily choices and shaping values, this percentage is shockingly high. In fact, it's only marginally higher for teenagers than it is for adults, suggesting that most people make relatively little progress on this crucial insight throughout the different stages in life. Faith and marriage are two factors that sometimes lead to an understanding of life purpose. Notice that married adults were somewhat less likely still to be searching for life's answers, while the never-been-marrieds were the most likely to be deliberating on this matter. The two previously married segments—the divorced and widowed—reflect a type of crisis in this regard, with some individuals in those categories renewing their quest for purpose after their marriage ended.

In terms of their sociopolitical views, most adults consider themselves to be moderate or middle-of-the-road in ideological matters. Again, this is a function of age and life stage more than marital status. One of the unexpected realities, though, is that young adults are more likely to embrace the somewhere-in-between ground than to portray themselves as politically liberal or conservative. Deeper probing reveals that this is because they feel ill-informed on most issues and thus balk at taking a definitive stand; they are loathe to embrace labels, feeling that such categorizations are limiting, inaccurate and irrelevant. As members of a generation that is comfortable with contradictions, they feel little kinship to either end of the ideological spectrum.

Divorce tends to move people more toward the political center and, in particular, away from the ideological right. The act of dissolving the relationship that they had counted on for stability, security and fulfillment raises numerous questions in the mind of divorced adults. The dissolution also facilitates a more profound sense of self-doubt and challenges their notion of how things work and what makes sense in life. One outgrowth of that self-doubt is a softening of their political views. Another consequence is a lessened likelihood of participating in the political process, which includes a diminished incidence of voting.

RELIGIOUS AND SPIRITUAL IMAGE

Over the past two decades, Americans have become increasingly comfortable with and curious about spirituality. People's spiritual views and experiences play a central role in defining their nature and life.

Not surprisingly, 4 out of 5 adults consider themselves Christian. Christianity has become a generic term over the past quarter century; it implies that someone is not associated with a non-Christian faith group rather than insinuating that they are a devoted follower of Jesus Christ.[1] Again, this self-perception is driven more by generation and life stage than by marital status. In table 2.6, you will notice that the segment with the greatest accumulation of young people (i.e., never-been-marrieds) is twice as likely as the older segments of the population to embrace the label "atheist" and is the least likely to adopt the label "Christian."

In like manner, spirituality is something that has greater appeal to older adults than to younger adults. All of the spiritual talk among young adults has confounded many cultural observers, leading them to posit that young adults are more spiritually inclined than their elders. However, this is not the case. Young adults are divided into two camps: those who are deeply spiritual and those who recognize the potentially significant role of spirituality but have, at least for the time being, rejected or shelved it. Those who are spiritually minded tend to be more intently focused on faith matters than young adults have been for the past two decades, although they are also somewhat less likely to pursue Christianity as their sole faith of choice. At the same time, a surprisingly large portion of the never-been-married group has rejected faith as a core life component and a viable means of self-description. Often, their distaste for religious experience and involvement stems from their sense that religious people and faith systems are either hypocritical or powerless. What is the driving force behind this conclusion? In many instances it is the divorce of their parents or of the parents of their closest friends, the ones who had made faith a visible cornerstone in their life.[2]

Most people who delve into the spiritual realm consider themselves deeply immersed in it. (Again, the exceptions to the rule are the younger adults.) This reflects the relative superficiality of American culture more than an intense affiliation with faith. Half of the never-been-married segment, nearly two-thirds of the married and divorced groups and three-fourths of the widowed niche contend that they are "deeply spiritual." As we will see in chapters 5, 6 and 7, this may be regarded as an overstatement of their spiritual commitment and depth. However, it is an important element to understand vis-à-vis how Americans see themselves. Most adults

> # IN REALITY, THE BULK OF OUR POPULATION IS MORE CONCERNED ABOUT "TOUCHING BASE" WITH THE SPIRITUAL DIMENSION THAN WITH "OWNING" THAT DIMENSION.

think of themselves as spiritual people. This self-image helps them to feel well-rounded, moral, vertically aligned and horizontally connected. In reality, the bulk of our population is more concerned about "touching base" with the spiritual dimension than with "owning" that dimension.

TABLE 2.6

THE RELIGIOUS SELF-IMAGE OF AMERICANS

Self-Description	SGL	NBM	WID	DIV	MAR
Christian	82%	78%	91%	85%	89%
Spiritual	71	65	74	76	76
Deeply spiritual	58	48	78	62	62
Born-again Christian	37	30	53	43	41
Atheist	8	10	4	6	5

Key: SGL=all single adults; NBM=never-been-married; WID=widowed; DIV=divorced; MAR=married.
Source: A national survey by the Barna Research Group, January 2001. The study randomly surveyed 1,005 adults, which included 504 single adults.

Another religious label that gets tossed around is "born-again Christian." At this juncture in our journey into the lives of single adults, we won't question the meaning of that term in the minds and hearts of those who embrace it (we will explore this issue more deeply in chapter 7). Recognize, however, that despite the often negative connotations associated with the label "born-again Christian," 3 out of 10 never-been-marrieds, 4 out of 10 divorced and married adults, and half of all widowed individuals adopt the term as an accurate self-description. The data also reveal that about half of widowed, divorced and married adults who view themselves as Christian embrace the label "born-again." This practice is less common within the never-been-married niche, among whom roughly 2 out of 5 self-professed Christians also think of themselves as being born again.[3]

A WAVY MIRROR

A colleague in ministry with whom I shared the self-portrait painted by single adults laughed in bemusement and asked, "Do you think that's really how they see themselves? They are really self-deluded, aren't they?" The answer to that question is not nearly as important as recognizing that there may very well be a substantial gap between how single adults see themselves and how married adults—like my friend—see them.

It is not uncommon to find that a person's self-view contrasts with the views of those who observe from afar. For those who wish to effectively work with single adults, whether as a friend, an employer, a family member or a representative of Christ, the challenge is not to correct those self-impressions but to understand them and work in tandem with those perceptions. "Maybe the best we can hope to do," explained a counselor to singles with whom I spoke, "is to hold up a mirror and help them see themselves in the most objective light possible. I can't change them and you can't change them—that's between themselves and God. Frankly, since any changes that you or I would initiate are subjective, based on our personal values and beliefs, changing them isn't a very hopeful enterprise and, sometimes, not a very healthy or beneficial venture for either party. We'd be better off understanding who they think they are and then helping them to clarify and evaluate that self-image, by working with them within the boundaries of that perception."

CHAPTER 3

HOW SINGLE
ADULTS LIVE

One overlooked joy of modern American life is watching our diversity play out in daily choices and activities. While most of us take such freedom and independence for granted, the range of choices and sheer unpredictability of people's behaviors and preferences can be both frustrating and exciting. And rarely does such rampant individuality lead to boredom. The idiosyncratic lifestyles of single adults are a prime example of Americans doing what they do best: being themselves.

Most Americans, regardless of their marital status or age, believe that the greatest challenge in life is to achieve happiness and fulfillment. In fact, we discovered that most adults contend that God blesses them so that they may experience a heightened sense of enjoyment and personal fulfillment in life. However, only a relative handful understand the Genesis 12 principle that we are blessed so that we might be a blessing to others. In other words, most people discount that servantlike perspective and instead focus on their personal goals, preferences and needs toward reaching happiness.

> MOST AMERICANS, REGARDLESS OF THEIR MARITAL STATUS OR AGE, BELIEVE THAT THE GREATEST CHALLENGE IN LIFE IS TO ACHIEVE HAPPINESS AND FULFILLMENT.

LIVING FOR HAPPINESS

You might be surprised to learn that a large majority of single adults— 64 percent, or roughly two-thirds—describe themselves as "extremely satisfied" or "very satisfied" with their life. You might be even more surprised to discover that this level of satisfaction pales in comparison to that measured among married adults, in which 9 out of 10 (90 percent) claim to be extremely or very satisfied with their life. Among single adults, widowed individuals have the highest levels of satisfaction (74 percent), trailed by the never-been-married niche (67 percent) and the divorced segment (55 percent).[1]

From these numbers, we can glean two insights: First, most single adults are generally pleased with the way their life is unfolding. Clearly, marriage is not required to live a fulfilling and pleasing life in America these days. Most single adults have figured out how to cope with the pressures and challenges of life with the help of family and friends and their own unique skills and abilities.

Second, single adults are likely to find that a healthy marriage will increase their joy in life. All three singles segments evidenced lower satisfaction levels than married adults. Even divorced and widowed adults (i.e., the formerly married) experienced declines in satisfaction. Naturally, the quality of one's marriage makes a big difference. A strong marriage may alleviate some of the biggest challenges that single adults face, but a rocky union often results in a divorce, and the numerous hardships that such dissolution produces include a sense of isolation and personal failure.

Happiness is a composite perspective, though, based upon a combination of attitudes pertaining to several core life dimensions. We discovered that single adults are most satisfied with their spiritual and emotional experiences, somewhat less at peace with their professional or occupational life and least satisfied with their material and financial experience. Further insight is gleaned by recognizing that when their satisfaction levels are compared with those of married adults, the biggest gaps emerge in connection with their emotional and relational undertakings (15 percentage points less satisfied than married adults) and their financial state (13 percentage points lower).[2]

CHECKING OUT THE CHECKBOOK

If it's true that you can tell the priorities in people's lives by examining their checkbooks, then the things that matter most to single adults are their home, their car and their stomach. Those three elements combined consume 3 out of every 5 dollars they earn. Relatively small amounts—anywhere from 2 percent to 5 percent of their aggregate earnings—are devoted to clothing, health care, transportation, entertainment, education and charitable contributions. Taxes consume nearly one-tenth of their income.[3]

Widowed adults allocate their incomes quite differently from other singles. These individuals—mostly elderly women—devote nearly half of their income to housing expenses. Health care, food and transportation each require an average of 13 percent of their earnings. Health care takes a deep bite out of their funds, consuming two-and-a-half times greater a percentage of their annual revenue than that of other single adults. Widowed adults eat a greater number of their meals at home than other singles, and never-been-marrieds and divorced people nearly split their meal money between home and eating out. Widowed adults also give away more money each year than never-been-marrieds or divorced individuals—even though the younger singles earn considerably more, on average, than do widowed folk. The significance of this commitment is underscored by the fact that the typical widowed adult dips into his or her savings each year, draining nearly $1,000 from their reserve to get by. In that light, their generosity is especially commendable.

The significant differences in priorities between married and single adults relate to housing, transportation and giving. Married individuals pay a smaller share of their total income for housing—only about one-quarter compared to about one-third among singles. Married people allocate more money for transportation but give away only half as much of their income as singles donate to churches and other nonprofit organizations. In fact, the average widowed adult donates three times more of his or her income to causes than do married couples. Relatively few single adults are wealthy, but they tend to donate a greater slice of their pie to those in need than do married couples.

EATING IS NOT ABOUT FOOD

The eating habits of most single adults leave a lot to be desired. Nutritionists claim that most singles—particularly the young, active, never-been-married group—make a habit of eating unbalanced meals. A recent Roper survey showed that only 1 in 4 single adults actually eat three meals a day; the norm is one or two meals supplemented by a series of snacks throughout the day. While this regimen is not necessarily harmful, the removal of home economics and life-skills classes from school curricula in recent years, as well as the diminished likelihood of parents teaching basic life skills to their children, has left millions of single adults without cooking skills, producing a nation of unmarried fast-food addicts. Research into consumer shopping patterns confirms that the days of cooking from scratch are long gone. Convenience, speed and ease are the "holy trinity" of food preparation these days. Singles spend less than a half hour in the grocery store on an average visit; grocery shopping is way down on the list of favorite things to do. The popularity of fast-cook and precooked meals has risen on a curve that parallels the growth of the single-adult population.

For many singles, eating is not about nutrition or the joy of cooking; it's about survival and relationships. Whenever possible, many single adults use meals as an opportunity to spend time with friends. The restaurant industry over the past few years has buzzed about the latest trend known as "dashboard dining," in which a small group of friends cram themselves into a car, head to the nearest fast-food joint and eat in the car while carrying on a riveting conversation. Believe it or not, this has become the third most popular type of eating experience among singles, trailing only a home-cooked meal and a convenience meal at home. As we will discuss, the factors that create these popular eating experiences are the provision of a unique or comforting experience and the ability to maintain and deepen relationships—two top priorities in the lives of singles.

> SINGLE ADULTS LOVE TO BE ENTERTAINED. ONE OF THE HALLMARKS OF OUR CULTURE IN THE INITIAL DECADE OF THE TWENTY-FIRST CENTURY IS OUR ADDICTION TO EXPERIENCES AND ADVENTURES.

ENTERTAINING SINGLE ADULTS

Even more than most Americans, single adults love to be entertained. One of the hallmarks of our culture in the initial decade of the twenty-first century is our addiction to experiences and adventures. Increasingly, we are adopting the postmodern notion that we work primarily to earn enough money to afford to play more frequently and more enjoyably. More than ever, we judge the value of our relationships and the organizations we participate in on the basis of the experiences they facilitate in our lives. Nowhere is this more evident than when we explore the lifestyles of single adults.

You can see it in their spending. Americans spend roughly 5 percent of their income on entertainment, regardless of their marital status. The areas in which singles spend more money than do married adults, in percentage terms, include reading materials, consumer electronics (excluding computers), entertainment events (largely music, sports and movies) and meals and drinks. Among the areas in which they spend less are computer software and accessories, outdoor activities and equipment, and magazines.

Reading is not a major entertainment form for young singles, but it becomes a dominant practice among the oldest singles, particularly widowed adults. Overall, singles are responsible for about 1 out of every 5 books purchased each year in America, spending an average of about $125 annually on books. Married and widowed adults are more likely to read for pleasure during a typical week than are younger singles (especially the never-been-married niche). The latter segment tends to read for educational or vocational reasons to a greater extent, as they are seeking to get ahead in their career and generate a more comfortable living. Many young singles consider reading to be an appropriate endeavor for retired people but not an activity for which they personally feel they can spare the time.

To a large extent, young singles substitute movies and videos for recreational reading. While they convince themselves that time is not available for reading, most singles perceive the hours spent watching movies and videos to be a wise entertainment investment. The typical never-been-married individual sees nearly one new movie per month at theaters and rents one or two additional movies per month. Older singles—especially widowed females—are less-avid movie buffs, visiting theaters only a handful of times during the course of the year. Among single adults, one-quarter never go to the theater.[4]

Additionally, listening to music is a major pastime for most single adults. Between the radio, music videos, CDs and audiocassettes, singles spend more time listening to music than any other activity, with the exception of sleeping, working and watching TV. Once again, though, a huge gap stands between the listening habits of never-been-marrieds, divorced and widowed adults. The devoted music lovers are the younger brood—the never-been-marrieds. More than three-quarters of that segment buys recorded music during the year, compared to 6 out of 10 divorced adults and just 3 out of 10 widowed adults. The types of music they buy vary considerably as well. Whereas never-been-married individuals are most likely to purchase rock, rap and R&B recordings, divorced adults most often select rock or country music, while widowed adults prefer Christian and country.

These purchases reflect the divergent musical tastes of each group. Table 3.1 allows us to compare the relative favorability of the major genres of music in the eyes of each singles niche. Among the never-been-married contingent, the genres that have more supporters than critics include R&B, pop, Christian, jazz and alternative rock. A greater portion of these adults dislike rap and country than enjoy them, while rock music gets a mixed rating (although most of the disapproval relates to heavy metal). Among widowed adults, the favored styles of music include Christian, country and classical, while the least enjoyed sounds include rap and rock (especially heavy metal). Divorced adults are the most eclectic group, leaning towards pop, Christian, country, R&B and jazz, while strenuously rejecting rap and also turning their backs on rock. To put this in context, married adults are most enamored of Christian, classical and country music while a majority chose rap as their least favorite genre, distantly followed by rock.

TABLE 3.1

FAVORED AND DISLIKED MUSICAL STYLES
OF SINGLES AND MARRIEDS

	Favorite Style of Music				Most Disliked Music Style			
Music Style	**NBM**	**WID**	**DIV**	**MAR**	**NBM**	**WID**	**DIV**	**MAR**
Rock	18%	8%	17%	18%	20%	27%	28%	32%
R&B	16	*	5	3	2	*	*	1
Rap/hip-hop	9	*	1	1	25	35	46	52
Pop	8	3	4	7	3	3	*	3
X	8	24	11	16	2	1	*	1
Country	6	20	18	14	22	8	10	9
Jazz	6	5	9	3	*	7	*	2
Dance/swing	4	4	3	2	2	1	2	1
Alternative	4	*	1	*	*	*	*	*
Classical	3	12	7	9	2	*	3	1
Latin	3	*	4	2	1	*	*	*

Key: NBM=never-been-married; WID=widowed; DIV=divorced; MAR=married.

* Indicates less than half of 1 percent.

Source: A national survey by the Barna Research Group, November 2000. The study randomly surveyed 1,005 adults.

INQUIRING MINDS

Single adults have varied levels of interest in current affairs, but a general pattern is evident: The older the people, the more likely they are to pay attention to news.

While singles most often rely upon network TV news, local TV news, daily newspapers and cable news networks, the relative importance of various information sources varies from singles niche to singles niche. Never-been-married individuals are more likely than their unmarried counterparts to turn to MTV, the Internet and morning TV magazine shows, and less likely to access newspapers, Sunday morning commentary TV programs and religious radio programs for insight. Widowed adults are more prone to seek out the local TV news and are less enamored of cable network news, MTV, late-night TV programs and the Internet. Divorced adults are more likely than others to glean insights from network TV news, weekly national news magazines, the daily news-paper, public TV and religious radio. They are less prone to consider sources such as MTV and the Internet.

In terms of raw appetite for news stories, the widowed population wins hands down, while never-been-married and divorced adults are gen-erally somewhat indifferent to the goings-on around the world. Single parents in particular make little effort to stay abreast of world affairs, largely due to the busyness of their days. In fact, the ability to catch up on the news without making major personal sacrifices is often a sign that indicates they have passed from the overloaded single-parent stage to the empty nest single-parent phase.

RELATING TO FRIENDS AND FAMILY

For most single adults, friends and extended family are central to their existence. For never-been-married adults, the "tribal" relationships exemplified in television shows such as *Friends* are common. Group activities remain popular, reducing the pressure on each individual to facilitate compelling outings consistently. Dating is widely viewed with trepidation, partially because the stakes are perceived to be high—find-ing a soul mate is no simple task—and partially because the process of dating is deemed to be expensive, awkward or frustrating. The housing situation for many never-been-marrieds is also surprising. One out of every 5 25- to 29-year-old men and 1 out of 10 30- to 34-year-old men, as well as 1 out of 12 women in the 25 to 29 age category, are still living at home with their parents. While this facilitates close ties with their aging parents, it also raises relational challenges unforeseen by most parents.

Divorced adults devote most of their relational time to interacting with their children and with their colleagues from work. Plunging into the dating scene is especially awkward for many divorced people. Although most of them eventually get remarried, a pattern usually fol-lows the divorce. After an average of 8 years of marriage, the couple divorces. Then they spend 2 to 3 years being conspicuously "out of the market," another 2 to 3 years casually dating and a year or so seriously dating a prospective mate; then they remarry. Most of these people speak of competing tensions as they strive to regain stability in their life. They struggle with the trauma of their shattered marriage, the heart-break of interacting with their children differently, the challenge of redefining themselves, the difficulty of thinking about dating again, the emotional highs and lows that accompany dating, the ecstasy of finding a potential mate, the self-doubts that plague their planning for the next phase of their life and so on.

Millions of divorced adults struggle to find equilibrium in their reshaped relationships with their children. The parent who gains custody of the children must usually juggle child-rearing duties with sole-breadwinner status. The parent who loses custody must adjust to the occasional scheduled visit. In 4 out of 5 cases, single moms are awarded primary custody of the kids; but in half of those households, the family lives on the brink of or in poverty. These parents are much more intentional than many married parents about the time they spend with their kids.

Widowed adults divide their time between extended family and peers they meet through the organizations in which they associate (e.g., churches, clubs and seniors associations). Relatively few widowed folk emerge from their time of grieving with a determination to remarry. Since the 1960s, large portions of the seniors segment have been moving into housing designed to meet their special needs and interests. Today, one-quarter of all senior citizens live in one of the nearly 30,000 assisted-living facilities throughout the country. Almost half of all elderly people will live in a nursing home, an assisted-care complex or some other type of residential care option. It is in these places that seniors—and especially widowed seniors, most of whom are female—build many of their new and significant friendships.

On a lighter note, many single adults share their life with a pet, although singles surprisingly are less likely to have a pet than are married adults. (To understand why, think kids.) In fact, married couples are two-and-a-half times more likely to own a dog, twice as likely to have a cat and twice as likely to own a bird than are single adults. Widowed adults are more likely to own household pets than are other singles, but even their rates of pet ownership are lower than those of family households.[5] Most single adults regard pets as another point of responsibility rather than a source of companionship.

HAVING SEX OUTSIDE OF MARRIAGE

Living in a society that is fascinated with sex, we should not be surprised to learn that the absence of marriage has failed to stop most single adults under the age of 50 from having regular sexual interludes. This practice is encouraged by contemporary marketing (which employs the "sex sells" philosophy of Madison Avenue), the rise of the postmodern worldview (there is no right or wrong, and only you can decide what's right and appropriate for yourself) and the mixed messages people receive while growing up (ranging from the idea that what you do with your body is completely up to you to the practice of safe sex to abstinence).

The consequence of our sexual obsession and lack of moral absolutes is that among 21-year-olds, fewer than 1 out of 5 are married, and more than 4 out of 5 have had sexual intercourse—most of them with more than 1 partner. There are a number of implications regarding this state of affairs. First, few people getting married for the first time are virgins. Sexual activity continues long after the teen years for most single women: 42 percent of single women under 45 have sexual intercourse during a typical year.[6] The figures are even higher among single men.

Second, such rampant sexual experimentation has led to America's performing more abortions than any other nation in the world. Thankfully, the number of known abortions has declined somewhat since the mid-90s; yet, we continue to sustain more than 25 abortions for every 100 live births. Among women under 25, the ratio is much higher, at more than 40 abortions for every 100 live births.[7] Eighty percent of all abortions are performed on single women.[8]

Third, the U.S. has the world's highest rate of pregnancy among unmarried teenagers and unmarried women. More than 1 million babies are born annually to unmarried women, which is more than one-quarter of the total live births in our country. This is most common in the black community, where 2 out of every 3 births are to single mothers. Among Hispanic women, 2 out of 5 births are to unwed mothers.[9] The Census Bureau notes that births outside of marriage continue to escalate, and the National Center for Health Statistics points out that births to unmarried women are most common among females 18 to 24 years of age. Although a large portion of children born to unwed mothers are not wanted, only 2 percent of those who are born are put up for adoption. Those children raised by their birth mother have a higher incidence of incurring child abuse, health crises, behavioral problems, substance abuse problems and academic underperformance.[10]

A final consequence worth noting is that the Centers for Disease Control report that 65 million Americans carry an incurable sexually transmitted disease (STD) and that an additional 15 million people are infected with such a disease each year. In total, they estimate that 1 out of every 4 teenagers already have an STD.

While the movement toward sexual abstinence in the past half decade has borne some positive fruit, the big picture shows that most single adults, even if they get through high school and the college years with their virginity intact, fall prey to sexual temptation once they enter the "real world."

WORKING MOTHERS

Government statistics indicate that a majority of mothers are now employed outside the home, at least part-time. As difficult as life is for the typical working mother, you can imagine how challenging and exhausting it is to be a single mom, 1 of the 8 million women who simultaneously serve as solo parent, chief breadwinner, head of the household and friend to others. Hard as they try to keep it all together, most single moms admit that they feel as if they are fighting a losing battle. The economic standing of these women typically supports their feelings. The median annual income for single mothers is barely $25,000—a solid 35 percent below the national household average. Among minority single moms, the picture is even worse: They average less than $20,000 annually, resulting in a majority of nonwhite children with unmarried mothers being raised below the poverty line.[11] This explains why more than 4 out of 5 married-couple families own their home, but the majority of single moms rent their residence.[12]

Single-parent women struggle to balance the multiple interests competing for their time and attention—not the least of which are their children. Exacerbating the challenge is the ever-escalating cost of raising a child these days. Estimates vary, but it is generally expected that raising a child born in 2000 through his or her seventeenth birthday will cost in the neighborhood of $165,000. For single mothers who are awarded alimony, the average award is barely $3,000 annually, and fewer than two-thirds of the designated recipients actually receive those payments. Despite the good intentions of the judicial system, holding down at least one full-time job is a must-do activity for single moms.

According to a single woman's life stage, work carries a variety of connotations. Among never-been-married women, jobs play a significant role in shaping identity, buttressing self-worth, securing independence and facilitating new relationships with people who will become lifelong friends and possibly a spouse. Single mothers of preteens, most of whom are in their 20s or 30s, consider their job to be a means to an end—in other words, a source of income enabling them to raise their children. For some of these mothers, work is also an escape from the runny noses and homework complaints that cause their seemingly permanent headaches. For older women, especially widowed females, holding down a job is less about economics and more about adding value to life and staying connected.

In the interest of fairness, single dads have a tough time, too. Although there are fewer single fathers with kids under 18 in their home—roughly 2 million—they still face many of the same struggles as their female counterparts. The one comparative advantage they have is financial stability. The median income of these fathers is almost $40,000, which is above the national household average. Though minority single fathers have a substantially lower median income than do white single dads (in the $30,000 to $33,000 range, depending on the ethnic group), they fare much better than minority single moms and even better than white single moms.[13]

INTEGRATING TECHNOLOGY

Increasingly, technology is central in the lifestyles of single adults. The typical household is now equipped with many of the recent technological advances, from microwave ovens (which are used by most never-been-married adults on a daily basis but are used by single moms less than any other segment of married or single adults) to cell phones and DVD players.[14] Most single adults rely upon these new products to save time, because time remains the primary obstacle that singles struggle to master.

Married-couple households are more likely than single-adult households to own most of the electronic technologies available today. This is not surprising given the spending levels of the different households on such equipment. While single adults tend to budget a higher percentage of their annual income for such devices (1.07 percent versus 1.03 percent respectively), their smaller revenue base frees up less total dollars for such purchases, thereby limiting the immediacy with which they can acquire new technology. The average $415 spent by singles to get their hands on the latest communications and entertainment equipment (excluding computers) is considerably lower than the $700 that married-couple households invest in similar products each year.[15]

VCRs have become one of the most universally owned pieces of household equipment, rivaling television sets in their ubiquity. Never-been-married adults, however, have led the way in adopting DVD players, perceiving that these new units will be the wave of the future and thus constitute a wiser investment of their limited household funds. Cell phones have become a necessary appendage, particularly among the highly relational never-been-marrieds. (Divorced and widowed adults have been slower to see the value of and to make the investment in cell phones.) Most singles have access to the Internet. Home-based access is more common among never-been-marrieds than the divorced and twice as common as among the widowed. The general pattern, then, is that never-been-married singles tend to sacrifice a bigger percentage of their income to have the latest and greatest technology, while divorced adults wait a while until prices come down and the technology becomes indispensable. Widowed adults typically remain impervious to the new developments, embracing them years after they have become commonplace in most homes. Many widowed adults maintain that they have lived a long and satisfying life without the new contraptions and believe that they can continue to live a fulfilling existence without such machines.

TABLE 3.2

HOUSEHOLD ELECTRONIC EQUIPMENT OWNED

Equipment	SGL	NBM	WID	DIV	MAR
VCR	91%	93%	78%	94%	96%
Cable TV	74	79	69	70	72
Cellular telephone	53	59	48	48	61
Desktop computer	48	52	34	50	63
CD-ROM in computer	45	51	26	51	60
Internet access on home computer	43	50	23	44	57
Internet access on nonhome computer	34	42	12	33	43
DVD player	19	23	16	15	18
Satellite dish for TV	17	18	15	17	21
Laptop/notebook computer	14	19	2	14	18
Palmtop computer	5	9	5	0	10

Key: SGL=all single adults; NBM=never-been-married; WID=widowed; DIV=divorced; MAR=married.
Source: A national survey by the Barna Research Group, January 2000. The study randomly surveyed 1,005 adults.

ACCESSING THE INTERNET

The Internet has taken the world by storm over the past decade, changing our lives more than any technology since the development of the television. As noted in table 3.2, accessing the Internet is a familiar if not integral activity for most singles, with the exception of widowed adults. Overall, two-thirds of all single adults have access to the Internet either at home or at work. Access peaks among the never-been-marrieds (7 out of 10), followed by the divorced (6 out of 10) and the widowed (fewer than 4 out of 10). For context, realize that 3 out of 4 married adults have Internet access, a rate slightly higher than that of the most connected singles niche.

Having access and using the Internet are two different elements, but the distinction is not significant in practical terms. Most people who have access to the Internet take advantage of it. Our research shows that among single adults, about half use the Internet at least once a week, about 1 out of 10 use it on a less frequent basis, and nearly 4 out of 10 never use it (which are almost exclusively the individuals who lack access). Never-been-marrieds are the most likely weekly users (two-thirds of them log on at least once a week), compared with about half of all divorced adults and only 1 out of 8 widowed individuals. In total, three-quarters of widowed people never go online; in fact, only one-third of those who have access bother to surf the information superhighway.

The most interesting insight into Internet usage relates to the functions that people turn to it to fulfill. The accompanying table indicates that across the board, people's most common use of the Internet is to locate specific information. Slightly more than 4 out of 10 single adults (and a slight majority of married people) rely upon the Internet to help maintain existing relationships and to buy products. Half of all never-been-married adults, 3 out of 10 divorced adults and one-quarter of married people use the Internet to examine new videos or to listen to music. Among the least common uses of the Internet by singles are to play video games (common among teenagers but not among adults), to participate in chat-room discussions (one-fourth of the never-been-marrieds engage in such activity compared to 1 in 10 divorced and married people), to make new friends (substantially more common among teens but undertaken by only one-sixth of singles) and to have a religious or spiritual experience (1 out of 10 single adults do so). Interestingly, divorced adults are twice as likely to use the Internet for religious purposes as are married adults, often because these individuals feel ostracized or unwelcome at churches as a result of their divorce.

TABLE 3.3

HOW SINGLE AND MARRIED ADULTS
USE THE INTERNET

Use of the Internet	SGL	NBM	DIV	MAR
Find information	96%	97%	96%	96%
Maintain existing relationships	43	44	47	55
Buy products	43	41	46	54
Check new music, videos	43	50	30	26
Play video games	27	28	26	18
Visit chat rooms	22	28	11	11
Make new friends	17	20	12	8
Have spiritual/religious experience	10	9	12	6

Key: SGL=all single adults; NBM=never-been-married; DIV=divorced; MAR=married.
Source: The Barna Institute, "The Cyberchurch," *Barna Research Online Home Page,* January 2001.
http://www.barna.org. The study explores the relationship of technology and faith, and likely developments in this regard in the future.

VARYING LIFESTYLES

One of the interesting observations from this review of single-adult lifestyles is that so much of what singles do relates directly to what they experienced growing up. The media they prefer, their sexual practices and values, personal spending habits, preferred music styles—all of these things and more become somewhat predictable by knowing a person's age and marital state. Be encouraged: It is quite possible to observe and understand these patterns and to convert that knowledge into sensitive and meaningful interaction.

CHAPTER 4

THE MATTERS OF THE HEART

A singles pastor recently told me, "Singles are just people. What's important about them isn't whether they have a husband or wife but what they think is important in life and how they pursue those things. All the talk about singleness is less important than diving beneath the surface and penetrating their hearts to perceive what motivates them. The last thing I want to hear about is the kind of person they want to marry—or avoid marrying again. What gets me involved in their life is understanding what they treasure, who they want to be and how they see themselves fitting into the world. I can't help them find a mate or find comfort in being single, but I can help them become all that God intended them to be—and that's fun!"

In other words, single adults are no different from anybody else. They're just people who are striving to understand themselves, their God, their world and their place in God's world. The best route to

> SINGLE ADULTS ARE NO DIFFERENT FROM ANYBODY ELSE. THEY'RE JUST PEOPLE WHO ARE STRIVING TO UNDERSTAND THEMSELVES, THEIR GOD, THEIR WORLD AND THEIR PLACE IN GOD'S WORLD.

empowering them to maximize their potential on this planet is to comprehend what matters in their hearts, which includes values, morals, goals and core attitudes. These elements define who they are, how they live and where they are going in life.

THE ROLE OF TRUTH

Knowing a person's heart requires an exploration of their foundational perspectives on what is right and wrong, what matters most and their source of wisdom in decision making. These elements combine to forge a person's worldview. The most significant element of people's worldviews and, thus, the cornerstone of their decision-making process, is their perspective on moral truth. Even though most Americans call themselves Christian, very few believe that absolute moral truth is conveyed by God through the Bible in order to direct our thinking and behavior. Most Americans—single or married, young or old, churchgoers or unchurched, born-again or not—contend that truth is relative to the individual and his or her circumstances. The consequence of such thinking is the condition in which we find America today—moral anarchy and chaos.

A majority of Americans are clearly confused about such matters and spend little time disentangling their thoughts on the issues involved. For instance, we find that half of all never-been-marrieds say they have no idea whether there is absolute moral truth or not, while two-thirds of those who have a position believe there are no moral absolutes. The picture is quite different among all single adults who have marriage experience (i.e., separated, divorced and widowed). Less than one-third do not have a position on moral truth, and those who have a perspective are comparatively more likely to argue that there are moral absolutes that do not change. Follow-up questions confirmed that a large percentage of adults who claim one position or another are not firmly convinced that their view is accurate.

TABLE 4.1

THE EXISTENCE OF MORAL ABSOLUTES

Moral Truth Perspective	SGL	NBM	WID	DIV	MAR
There are moral truths or principles that are absolute; they do not change according to the circumstances.	31%	18%	45%	44%	45%
There are no moral truths or principles that are absolute; moral truth always depends upon the situation or circumstances.	30	32	34	25	27
I have not thought about it. I have thought about it but don't know what to believe.	39	50	22	31	29

Key: SGL=all single adults; NBM=never-been-married; WID=widowed; DIV=divorced; MAR=married.
Sources: A national telephone sampling regarding morality by the Barna Research Group, May 2001. The study randomly interviewed 1,005 adults by telephone. Additional analysis of the data is available from the following two sources: Barna Research Group, "Practical Outcomes Replace Biblical Principles as the Moral Standard," *Barna Update*, September 10, 2001. http://www.barna.org (accessed 2001); Barna Research Group, "Morality in America," *Barna Research Online Home Page*. http:// www.barna.org (accessed 2001).

However, approaching the matter of truth from a different angle provides an entirely different outcome. When asked to identify the basis on which they make moral and ethical choices from day to day, people seem to have changing and relative foundations. Ironically, even people who perceive their choices to be founded on absolute beliefs can have changing and relative foundations.

TABLE 4.2

THE BASIS OF PEOPLE'S MORAL AND ETHICAL DECISIONS

Basis of Moral and Ethical Decisions	SGL	NBM	WID	DIV	MAR
Do whatever feels right/comfortable in a given situation	28%	29%	23%	25%	21%
Follow principles/standards based on the values your family taught you	15	13	11	21	19
Do whatever produces the best/most beneficial outcome for you personally	12	16	10	7	5
Do whatever will make people happy	10	8	12	7	7
Follow principles/standards based on the Bible	10	7	14	11	22
Follow principles/standards based on your feelings	7	5	4	11	7
Follow principles/standards based on your religious or church teachings (but not specifically the Bible)	6	2	5	8	11
Follow principles/standards based on your past observations and experience	6	6	7	10	6
Do whatever your family and friends expect	4	4	6	1	3

Key: SGL=all single adults; NBM=never-been-married; WID=widowed; DIV=divorced; MAR=married.
Source: A national survey by the Barna Research Group, July through November 2001. The study randomly surveyed 2,011 adults, which included 970 single adults. Of these single adults, 543 had never been married, 159 were widowed and 238 were currently divorced.

Overall, about 1 out of every 4 single adults base moral and ethical decisions on what feels right or feels most comfortable in a situation. Similarly, about one-eighth of singles—ranging from 7 percent of the divorced to 16 percent of the never-been-married—decide on the basis of personal benefits from the decision. One out of 10 seeks to avoid conflict with others, basing their choices on what will make others happy or placated.

Close to half of all single adults base their moral choices on set standards and principles, but the nature of those standards and principles varies considerably, as does the percentage of each singles niche that relies on such standards. In total, just 1 out of 3 never-been-marrieds turns to such standards, compared with two-fifths of widowed adults, three-fifths of divorced adults and two-thirds of married adults.

OVERALL, ABOUT 1 OUT OF EVERY 4 SINGLE ADULTS BASE MORAL AND ETHICAL DECISIONS ON WHAT FEELS RIGHT OR FEELS MOST COMFORTABLE IN A SITUATION.

Even more disparity emerges when identifying the content of those shaping principles. For instance, slightly fewer than 1 in 10 never-been-married adults (9 percent) turn to the Bible or teaching from their church or religious experiences. Twice as many widowed and divorced adults (19 percent) rely on faith-based guidance. Clearly, however, relatively few single adults turn to their faith to shape their moral and ethical choices. Feelings, social expectations and personal benefit are the driving forces behind the moral choices of most singles.

Realize that most unmarried people—or married individuals, for that matter—do not wrestle with issues of truth and morality. In fact, just 1 out of every 5 never-been-marrieds and 2 out of 5 previously married singles, as well 2 out of 5 currently married adults, contend that knowing about moral truth is very important. To most Americans, life is fast paced, complex, challenging and ever changing. Most Americans believe that it's important simply to do your best and then move on without obsessing over what's right and wrong (since most people aren't even sure such realities exist) and without wasting much time analyzing your choices. After all, Americans reason that there's too much to do to worry about the implications of past choices.

IDEOLOGY AND POLITICAL PARTICIPATION

Single adults are located at a different place on the ideological and philosophical continuum than are married people. First, individuals who have been married—whether they are currently married, divorced or widowed—are about 30 percent more likely to be registered voters than are people who have never been married. (Whereas 17 out of every 20 people with marriage experience are registered voters, only 13 out of 20 never-been-marrieds fit the same description.) This disparity is largely related to one's sense of responsibility. Being younger, having fewer people rely upon them and possessing a greater sense of independence and friskiness in life, never-been-marrieds are less prone to follow social and political issues, to feel a sense of impact and to take their personal responsibility in the democratic process as seriously as older, more established Americans do.[1]

Involvement in the political process differs too. One-third of married adults are registered Democrats, but close to half of all single adults claim that affiliation. Two-fifths of married people are registered Republicans, compared with only one-quarter of all singles. This orientation suggests that single adults are sufficiently in tune with political perspectives to recognize that the Democratic party is portrayed as more sensitive to the needs of the less affluent and less influential people groups, which is a self-view that singles of all types would embrace. The fact that divorced and widowed individuals are more prone to align with the Democratic party underscores the awareness possessed by the formerly married adults of the groups that most overtly proclaim an interest in advancing the cause of single adults.

The ideological differences of single and married adults are perhaps best illustrated by examining their philosophical self-descriptions, levels of voting participation and candidate preferences. Never-been-married people are much more likely to associate with liberal ideology. As a group, they are evenly divided between describing themselves as either "mostly liberal" or "mostly conservative" on social and political issues. Divorced adults definitely lean toward the "mostly conservative" label, while widowed and married people are three times more likely to describe themselves as conservative rather than liberal.

Voting turnout amplifies these same differences. In the 1998 national elections, in which a presidential race was not involved, the "more single" a person was, the lower was their likelihood of voting. Only 26 percent of never-been-marrieds voted, compared to 38 percent of divorced adults, 47 percent of widowed adults and 50 percent of married voters.[2] Similarly, in the 2000 presidential election, the same pattern emerged. Never-been-marrieds were the least likely voters, divorced adults were somewhat more likely to have cast a ballot, and widowed and married individuals were the most prolific voters.

The choice of candidates in the presidential election followed a completely different pattern. A majority of each of the single adult niches supported Democratic contender Al Gore, while a majority of married adults sided with Republican candidate George W. Bush. Oddly, the ideological leanings of each people group were a weak predictor of their candidate preference. Never-been-marrieds, who lean liberal, were marginally more likely to have voted for Gore than for Bush. Divorced individuals were twice as likely to support Gore as Bush. Widowed adults, one of the more conservative segments, decisively swung toward Gore. Married adults were the only group among these to push Bush, and they did so by about a 3-to-2 margin.

So what do these confusing patterns teach us? Simply that single adults are not an easy group to understand. And it is often because they do not understand (or accept) themselves and their present state of being. They are influenced by a variety of sources, making it hard to derive a black-and-white picture of who they are, what they think and how they behave. As was noted earlier, increasing numbers of Americans are comfortable with contradictions, even when the paradox in question relates to their own behavior!

Keep in mind that age and life stage remain dominant influences on people's thinking and behavior. Never-been-marrieds—often young adults—possess some generational traits that influence much of their behavior. They are comfortable with contradictions, independent in their behavior and unpredictable in their choices. They are inconsistently involved in causes, even those in which their views and behaviors would lead observers to expect them to be deeply invested. Divorced people are walking the balancing act between thinking and acting like a single person as opposed to a married adult. Widowed individuals remain, in their minds, married; it's simply that their spouse is no longer living with them. Yet, they have to behave like a single person in many ways, causing frequent cognitive dissonance and role confusion.

GOALS AND ASPIRATIONS

The goals we set for ourselves are driven by a combination of factors such as age, life experiences, education, worldview, faith commitment and life stage. Consequently, as we examine the priorities and future dreams of single adults, there is tremendous variation in terms of their life direction.

As the figures in table 4.3 indicate, never-been-married adults are focused mostly on maintaining their health, having close friends, living with integrity, getting married for life and having a comfortable lifestyle. Widowed people are focused on health, life's purpose, their relationship with God, spending time with family and remaining single. Divorced individuals have fewer driving goals for their lives than their single counterparts. Health is a major issue for them, followed by having close friends, a clear life purpose and a solid relationship with God.

Unique differences among these three singles populations become even more evident when you explore their secondary strata of goals. For the never-been-married group, achieving a clear sense of their life's purpose heads the second echelon of goals, followed by having a college degree, enjoying a satisfying sexual relationship with their partner, having a close relationship with God and remaining close to family. Some of the outcomes that did not make the cut included being deeply committed to the Christian faith (only 4 out of 10 see that as an attractive goal), having children (slightly less than half see this as very desirable), making a difference in the world and influencing people's lives, traveling extensively, owning the latest technology and achieving fame or public recognition.

TABLE 4.3

PERSONAL GOALS

Life Outcomes Deemed "Very Desirable"	SGL	NBM	WID	DIV	MAR
Experiencing good physical health	88%	84%	88%	96%	93%
Having close personal friendships	75	76	66	77	75
Living with a high degree of integrity	74	76	67	69	87
Having a clear understanding of the meaning and purpose of your life	72	70	76	72	78
Getting and staying married to the same partner for the duration of your life	70	78	72	53	88
Having a comfortable lifestyle	67	73	59	59	57
Having a close relationship with God	67	61	77	72	74
Living close to family/relatives	61	57	76	57	60
Having a satisfying sexual relationship with your marriage partner	55	64	40	50	69
Being deeply committed to the Christian faith	49	39	68	54	58
Having a college degree	49	64	38	29	35
Having children	48	46	43	51	61
Being knowledgeable about current events	46	42	52	43	52
Making a difference in the world	44	43	47	42	49
Being active in a church	40	34	60	39	45
Having a high-paying job	38	46	17	39	22
Influencing people's lives	35	39	30	26	39
Traveling throughout the world	29	29	26	29	23
Owning a large home	25	28	24	17	16
Owning latest technology/electronics	11	11	2	16	7
Achieving fame or public recognition	7	7	2	5	5

Key: SGL=all single adults; NBM=never-been-married; WID=widowed; DIV=divorced; MAR=married.
Source: A national survey by the Barna Research Group, January 2000. The study randomly surveyed 1,005 adults, which included 469 single adults. Of these single adults, 244 had never been married, 83 were widowed, and 123 were currently divorced.

Widowed folks have radically redefined what's important in life, given their typically advanced age and life experience. Beyond their top-rated goals, secondary goals include being deeply committed to Christianity, living with integrity, having good friends, being active in a church, living comfortably and staying up-to-date on world affairs. Among the items that are irrelevant to most widowed people are sex, education, influence, travel and household gadgets.

The divorced niche has yet a different spin on what's meaningful for their life. The secondary goals that drive them include living with integrity and comfort, living close to family, having a deep commitment to Christianity and having a fulfilling sexual relationship with a marriage partner. About half of all divorced individuals apparently look forward to remarriage, while the other half expect to remain single for the duration of their lives. Outcomes that do not get divorced adults excited include furthering their education, staying current on world affairs, being active in a church, having influence, traveling the world, owning the latest in consumer electronics and achieving fame.

Several intriguing patterns emerge from these figures. One relates to people's prioritization of their faith. Notice that each of the groups studied rated a personal relationship with God to be more important than being active in a church. However, the relative importance of church involvement varied. Only about half of the never-been-marrieds and divorced adults who prioritize a relationship with God also plan to pursue an active church life. That was considerably lower than the 6 out of 10 married adults and 8 out of 10 widowed adults who held the same conviction.

Another interesting insight is the relative loss of intensity that divorced adults seem to possess regarding their future. While at least 6 out of 10 never-been-married, widowed and married adults identified nine goals they deem very desirable, divorced adults only identified five. The average percentage of adults who listed the seven highest-ranked outcomes was also substantially lower among divorced adults than for any other group. Divorce affects people's life dreams and expectations in major ways.

A final revelation of importance is the relative disinterest that the youngest singles, mostly comprised of those who have yet to marry, have in relation to faith development. Young people traditionally rate faith items lower than do older adults, and the level of difference between the young and the old is becoming larger as time goes on. The fact that fewer than 2 out of 5 young adults desire to be deeply committed to the Christian faith, and that only 1 in 3 wants to be active in a church, sends a significant signal to church leaders about what lies ahead for congregations over the next two decades. This information fits the pattern we have recently identified among teenagers and adolescents who also have an interest in spiritual matters but little interest in an organized church.[3]

TABLE 4.4

THE RANKING OF PEOPLE'S GOALS

Life Outcomes Deemed "Very Desirable"	NBM	WID	DIV	MAR
Experiencing good physical health	1	1	1	1
Having close personal friendships	3t	8	2	5
Living with a high degree of integrity	3t	7	5	3
Having a clear understanding of the meaning and purpose of your life	6	3t	3t	4
Getting and staying married to the same partner for the duration of your life	2	5	9	2
Having a comfortable lifestyle	5	10	6	11
Having a close relationship with God	9	2	3t	6
Living close to family/relatives	10	3t	7	9
Having a satisfying sexual relationship with your marriage partner	7t	14	11	7
Being deeply committed to the Christian faith	15	6	8	10
Having a college degree	7t	15	16	15
Having children	11t	13	10	8
Being knowledgeable about current events	14	11	12	12
Making a difference in the world	13	12	13	13
Being active in a church	16	9	14t	14
Having a high-paying job	11t	16	14t	16

Key: NBM=never-been-married; WID=widowed; DIV=divorced; MAR=married.
t Indicates a tie
Source: A national survey by the Barna Research Group, January 2000. The study randomly surveyed 1,005 adults.

VALUES WORTH LIVING FOR

Describing people's worldviews and values gives us a sense of what's important and compelling to them. Furthermore, research provides us with additional insights into how single adults convert those perspectives on truth and righteousness into practical ideas and actions.

If there is any doubt that the moral condition of the nation is crumbling, a series of surveys dispels any such doubts. One such project, conducted among teenagers and college students by Peter Hart Research, found that 58 percent of teens and 52 percent of college students believe they have lower moral standards than do their parents, while only 15 percent of teenagers and 13 percent of college students say they possess higher moral standards than do their parents.[4] Even though morality gets a lot of media and pulpit attention across the country, and expressions of moral concern have risen dramatically in national polls during the past decade, only 1 out of 10 unmarried adults listed morality as the most important priority for our political leaders to tackle.[5]

The Role of Sex

You cannot understand Americans unless you comprehend the role of sex and sexuality in their life. Like evaluating a finely cut diamond, there are numerous facets to such insight, some of which are easier to see and interpret than others.

Cohabitation. Cohabitation plays a role in this examination. Presently, there is a huge gap between the attitudes of single adults and married adults on this issue. Three out of 4 never-been-married adults contend that cohabitation is morally acceptable, while a smaller majority of marriage-experienced singles (62 percent of divorced adults and 56 percent of widowed adults) and a large minority of married adults concur.[6]

If actions speak louder than words, then consider this: Three times as many single adults are cohabiting today as 20 years ago.[7] A majority of couples live together before getting married these days, which is a substantial increase from the 10 percent who did so in 1965. Sadly, while a majority of cohabiters do so in an effort to improve the chances of their potential union lasting the course of time, statistics show that cohabiters have a 48 percent greater chance of experiencing a divorce than do individuals who did not live together prior to marriage.[8] Cohabiters who eventually marry are also more likely to be victims of domestic violence, depression, dissatisfaction with life, shorter life spans and sexual anxiety.[9] In spite of all of these facts, a growing majority of young people (6 out of 10) believe that cohabitation is a good idea.[10]

Pregnancy. Giving birth to children outside of marriage is not necessarily an accident of careless sexual activity. One recent survey reports that a majority of 20-somethings contend that having a child without being married is "a worthwhile lifestyle" choice.[11] Among cohabiters who have a child, the percentage who marry after the pregnancy has declined from 57 percent in 1987 to just 44 percent in 1997.[12] One-third of all births each year are to unmarried women, the highest percentage of live births to single parents among any developed nation in the world. While most unmarried people take medical precautions to avoid an unwanted pregnancy, the one precaution that most of them refuse to adopt is abstinence.

Abortion. One of the dominant "solutions" to an unexpected or unwanted pregnancy is abortion. As noted earlier in the book, Americans have more than 1 million abortions every year. The Centers for Disease Control and the Alan Guttmacher Institute have been tracking abortions for years. Their information indicates that 8 out of 10 legal abortions are performed on single women, and two-thirds of all of these procedures are among never-been-married females. Six out of 10 women who have an abortion are white, and 53 percent of all abortions are performed on women who have not yet reached their twenty-sixth birthday. The most common reasons for having a baby aborted are predictable but chilling. Three-fourths say that having the baby would interfere with work, school or other responsibilities, two-thirds say they cannot afford to raise a child, and half do not want to be a single parent or have additional conflict with their partner. Abortion is almost always a decision of convenience rather than necessity. Just 15,000 of the 1.25 million or more abortions each year involve a case of rape or incest.[13]

Despite being a high-profile and controversial issue since the Supreme Court opened the door for legal abortions a quarter century ago, millions of Americans still flip-flop on this issue. Among never-been-marrieds, half describe themselves as pro-choice, 4 out of 10 say they are pro-life, and 1 out of 10 avoids such labels. About half support legal abortions either in most or all cases, while one-quarter say they should be permitted only in a few special situations, and 1 in 5 wants all abortions outlawed. Divorced adults are evenly divided between those who call themselves pro-life and pro-choice. Four out of 10 prefer legalizing abortions in all or most situations; one-third favor severe limitations on abortions; and one-sixth want to make all abortions illegal. Just less than half of all widowed adults support legal abortions in all or most circumstances, while one-quarter favor limited legality and one-quarter support outlawing it completely.

TABLE 4.5

VIEWS ON ABORTION

Perspective on Legalizing Abortion	SGL	NBM	WID	DIV	MAR
Should be legal in all/most circumstances	51%	55%	44%	42%	37%
Should be legal in only a few circumstances	28	25	28	36	36
Should be illegal in all circumstances	19	18	24	17	23
Moral Acceptability of Having an Abortion					
It is morally acceptable.	44	50	39	35	34
It is morally unacceptable.	48	45	51	51	55
Self-Description on Abortion Issues					
Consider self to be pro-choice	52	58	40	44	43
Consider self to be pro-life	37	34	42	41	49

Key: SGL=all single adults; NBM=never-been-married; WID=widowed; DIV=divorced; MAR=married.
Source: A national survey by the Barna Research Group, May 2001. The study randomly surveyed 1,003 adults.

Americans tend to set a more rigid personal standard than they want reflected in the law of the land. This is evident regarding abortion. It appears that most adults, including singles, want the laws to provide more latitude than they themselves would take advantage of. As for the moral appropriateness of abortion, half of the never-been-marrieds claim that it is morally acceptable, compared with just 4 out of 10 widowed adults and one-third of the divorced niche. (Overall, one-third of married adults deem abortion to be morally acceptable.) Along the same lines, a small majority of single adults favored FDA approval of the controversial French "abortion pill," officially known as RU-486.[14]

Pornography. One of the growing challenges in the area of sexuality is pornography. Pornography on the Internet has become a multibillion-dollar industry in the span of just a few years. Add the continuing revenues from other purveyors of such material and the porn industry emerges as a $10-billion-plus sector.

Although millions of parents are anguished about the potential of their children viewing unsolicited pornographic material on the Internet or in their e-mail, as well as about the ease with which their offspring can access such material online, most singles contend that it is morally acceptable for adults to view sexually explicit matter.

Movies are the pornography medium given the greatest leeway by adults. While only one-fifth of widowed adults think that movies that show explicit sex or nudity are morally acceptable, that figure doubles among married adults. A slim majority of divorced people and two-thirds of never-been-marrieds suggest that such movies are morally acceptable. Pornographic magazines are slightly less permissible in the eyes of single people. Oddly, more widowed people feel porn magazines are acceptable than are sexually explicit movies. In addition, fewer singles (one-third of the married, less than half of the divorced and a little over half of the never-been-married) deem skin magazines morally acceptable than is true regarding sexually explicit movies.

TABLE 4.6   **VIEWS ON PORNOGRAPHY**

Perspective on Pornography	**SGL**	**NBM**	**WID**	**DIV**	**MAR**
Watching a movie with explicit sex or nudity					
Morally acceptable	56%	67%	21%	53%	45%
Not morally acceptable	41	31	74	43	51
Reading a magazine with explicit sexual pictures or nudity					
Morally acceptable	52	62	29	46	36
Not morally acceptable	46	37	68	52	61

Key: SGL=all single adults; NBM=never-been-married; WID=widowed; DIV=divorced; MAR=married.
Source: A national survey by the Barna Research Group, May 2001. The study randomly surveyed 1,003 adults.

Harboring sexual thoughts or fantasies about someone other than a spouse bothers relatively few people. Widowed adults were the only segment who were more likely to consider sexual fantasies morally unacceptable rather than morally acceptable. But even among them, less than half said such thoughts were illegitimate. Three out of 5 divorced people and three-quarters of the never-been-married contingent felt that such fantasies were morally acceptable.

Homosexuality. One of the most controversial public issues of the day is that of gay rights. The increasing number of people who believe that homosexuality is something that you are born with, rather than a conscious behavior that is chosen, is slightly more than one-third of all single adults. This is up from fewer than 1 in 10 just a decade ago, which indicates people's attitudes on this issue are in a state of flux and further change in people's views on the matter is likely.

Homosexuality is an issue on which the generational divide is most evident. Two-thirds of never-been-married individuals say homosexuality is an acceptable alternative lifestyle, which is nearly double the percentage of widowed people who hold this view and considerably more than the 44 percent of divorced people and 39 percent of married adults who concur. The gap is even wider regarding the legality of homosexual relations between consenting adults. Seven out of 10 never-been-marrieds sanction gay relationships, while just less than half of divorced and married adults and only one-third of widowed adults agree. Perhaps surprisingly, there is much less support for clergy performing marriage ceremonies for gay couples or blessing those unions. Again, the never-been-married segment is most supportive of this notion, but less than half endorse the idea, while only 1 out of 4 other single and married adults favor such clergy involvement. Among divorced adults, the idea is rejected by a 2-to-1 margin, while widowed adults disapprove by a 3-to-1 margin.

Again, people were more likely to endorse legal permission for homosexual relationships than to define them as moral. Just 4 out of 10 never-been-marrieds, one-fourth of divorced adults and 1 out of 8 widowed people said a sexual relationship between two consenting people of the same gender is morally acceptable. (One out of 4 married adults took that side as well.)

TABLE 4.7   VIEWS ON HOMOSEXUALITY

Perspective on Homosexuality	SGL	NBM	WID	DIV	MAR
Homosexuality between consenting adults					
Should be legal	58%	69%	35%	46%	44%
Should not be legal	33	25	47	41	46
Homosexuality as an alternative lifestyle					
Should be considered acceptable	54	63	35	44	39
Should not be considered acceptable	39	33	49	44	52
You are born homosexual	37	37	36	35	35
You become homosexual due to external factors	46	48	38	47	48
Clergy should perform/bless gay marriages	37	45	22	27	26
Clergy should not perform/bless gay marriages	53	48	67	60	67
A sexual relationship with a person of same sex					
Morally acceptable	32	39	13	24	22
Not morally acceptable	66	59	88	74	75

Key: SGL=all single adults; NBM=never-been-married; WID=widowed; DIV=divorced; MAR=married.
Source: A national survey by the Barna Research Group, May 2001. The study randomly surveyed 1,003 adults.

Divorce

On the issue of divorce, most Americans want marital dissolution to be more difficult. By a 3-to-1 margin, adults are more likely to support making a divorce more difficult to obtain. There are extenuating circumstances that some people would take into account, most notably the presence of children in the family. About one-third of all adults believe that a couple that has an unsatisfying marriage should remain together simply for the sake of their children.[15] A study from the University of Chicago found that men are much more likely to engage in adultery than are women, but most Americans contend that they have never engaged in adultery.[16] Most alarming, though, is the finding in another study of unmarried 20-somethings in which two-thirds of the males and about half of the women would have sex with someone they found attractive, even though they had no interest in marrying them; and half of the men and one-third of the women in that same age group believe it's acceptable to have sex with someone they really like, even if they only know the other person for just a brief time.[17]

Not quite 1 out of every 4 adults, regardless of their marital status, say that if a couple gets divorced for a reason other than adultery, they have committed a sin. Perhaps this sentiment is driven by the widespread notion that although divorce is undesirable, it is almost inevitable these days. If current trends hold true, a majority of newly married couples are likely to get divorced, an outcome that will not surprise too many Americans. One-quarter of all singles and one-fifth of married people say divorce is likely, while another two-thirds believe a marriage has nothing better than a 50-50 chance of survival.

Thankfully, most people still acknowledge that an extramarital affair is morally unacceptable. More than 9 out of 10 singles submit that a married person having an affair with another married person is a morally unacceptable act. Three out of 4 never-been-married and widowed adults and two-thirds of the divorced niche contend that a married person having an affair with an unmarried person is also morally unacceptable. (The survey did not probe the matter, but one must wonder if the fact that many more divorced people find affairs with unmarried people morally permissible is because it was that very activity that destroyed their own marriage.) It is also noteworthy that unmarried adults are more than twice as likely as married adults to find an affair between a married and unmarried person morally legitimate.

TABLE 4.8

VIEWS ON ADULTERY AND DIVORCE

Perspective on Adultery and Divorce	SGL	NBM	WID	DIV	MAR
Divorce, except in cases of adultery					
Is a sin	24%	25%	22%	22%	28%
Is not a sin	69	70	67	67	61
A married person having an affair with a married person other than their spouse					
Is morally acceptable	6	7	4	6	5
Is not morally acceptable	93	92	93	94	94
A married person having an affair with an unmarried person					
Is morally acceptable	26	23	22	32	11
Is not morally acceptable	72	74	75	65	86

Key: SGL=all single adults; NBM=never-been-married; WID=widowed; DIV=divorced; MAR=married.
Source: A national survey by the Barna Research Group, May 2001. The study randomly surveyed 1,003 adults.

Substance Abuse

One of the best indicators of Americans' struggle with the notion of morality is evident by looking at their view on alcohol abuse. Most people would contend that excessive drinking has the potential to turn ugly, but surprisingly few young people are prepared to cast drunkenness as a corrupt behavior. A slight majority of never-been-marrieds say that getting drunk is morally acceptable. Just 1 out of 10 widowed people and 3 out of 10 divorced adults concur.

Drug abuse remains a hot issue in the U.S. Both single and married people harbor serious concerns about drug use. Nine out of 10 adults believe the country has a serious drug abuse problem to address, and about half of all adults (single as well as married) say the drug problem is serious in their own neighborhoods. It may seem odd, then, to learn also that half of all adults argue that too many people are put in jail simply for possession of narcotics. This is partially explained, though, by the fact that single adults are twice as likely to say that drug abuse should be treated more as a disease than a criminal offense.[18] (Married adults are evenly split on that score.)

The recent debates about using marijuana for purposes other than medicinal treatments also raised some marked differences of opinion. Seven out of 10 single adults believe doctors should be allowed to prescribe marijuana to their patients for medicinal purposes. Singles are also evenly divided on whether or not the possession of small amounts of marijuana used for recreational purposes should be a criminal offense. (A slight majority of married adults lean toward making possession of any amount illegal.)[19] Once again, many singles are willing to legalize behaviors that they perceive to be morally unacceptable. In this case, a little more than one-third of all never-been-marrieds believe nonmedicinal marijuana use is morally acceptable, compared with one-quarter of the divorced and one-seventh of the widowed populations.[20]

INTEGRITY

Integrity is the uncompromising adherence to moral and ethical principles. In light of this definition, remember that most single adults do not believe in the existence of moral absolutes. This contrast between the traditional and contemporary views of integrity helps to explain the widespread embrace of attitudes and behaviors that have historically been deemed inappropriate or immoral.

> A GOOD EXAMPLE OF THE DECLINE OF MORAL INTEGRITY IS THE FACT THAT 6 OUT OF 10 SINGLE ADULTS SAY THAT SOMETIMES IT IS NECESSARY TO LIE JUST TO GET BY.

A good example of the decline of moral integrity is the fact that 6 out of 10 single adults say that sometimes it is necessary to lie just to get by. Another reality is that just 1 out of 10 singles say that it is morally acceptable to cheat on income tax filings, while 2 out of 10 admit to having done so in the past.[21] And how about the discovery that one-quarter of all never-been-marrieds say it is morally acceptable knowingly to keep excess change you receive by mistake at a store? (Just 1 out of 10 widowed adults and 1 out of 20 divorced people hold the same view.) One out of 7 widowed adults and 1 out of 8 never-been-married people say that lying on a resume, if it will improve the chances of getting a job, is morally acceptable.[22]

Among the most clear-cut departures from traditional moral perspectives come in relation to never-been-marrieds and the issues of profanity and speeding. In both cases, a majority of these predominantly young people call intentionally breaking the speed limit and the use of profane language morally acceptable behaviors. Again, this is generational rather than marital in genesis. One-quarter of widowed and divorced adults view profanity as morally defensible, while 4 out of 10 divorced folks and only 15 percent of the widowed niche argue that speeding is morally acceptable behavior.[23]

FINAL THOUGHTS

These perspectives provide an insider's glimpse into what makes unmarried people tick. In some cases they are no different than married people. Sometimes their behaviors are influenced more by life stage or generation than by their marital state. In other cases they are radically different in their views and actions.

It also bears noting that the moral sensibilities of a substantial number of single adults seem rather warped. For instance, four times as many widowed adults are likely to say that abortion is morally acceptable as they are to say that getting drunk is acceptable. Divorced adults are more likely to condone pornography, homosexuality and cohabitation than drunkenness. The never-been-married folks in our nation are more prone to endorse pornography, cohabitation, abortion and homosexuality than to support drunkenness or stealing (i.e., keeping excess pocket change from a grocery store). And the reasoning is simple: Lacking any moral standard as a basis for such considerations, the final determination of right and wrong is personal and conditional. The result is an unusual and unpredictable scrabble of values and behaviors.

CHAPTER 5

THE ROLE OF FAITH

Americans are known for their interest in religion, which became even more evident after the September 11 terrorist attacks in 2001. While spirituality and talk about God were on the hearts and minds of the nation, not everyone perceived America's resurgence of faith to have influenced people's lives in a God-glorifying way.

Plenty of evidence exists to suggest that faith is an important influence in Americans' lives. Even single adults who may be somewhat diverted to other interests still allow faith to play a significant role in their lives. Two out of 3 never-been-married people say they are "spiritual." In addition, half of those who have never walked down the aisle describe themselves as "deeply spiritual." The numbers are even higher for the rest of the singles niches. Three-quarters of both widowed and divorced adults say they are "spiritual." Three-fifths of the divorced and three-quarters of the widowed describe themselves as "deeply spiritual." (Among the widowed, it's an all-or-nothing deal—either you're deeply spiritual or you're not.)

But apart from thinking that singles are spiritually inclined, how does faith work itself into their hearts and minds?

WHAT'S MY OPINION?

Most single adults possess sufficient knowledge of the major faiths to have developed some lasting impressions of each faith group. For the most part, Americans are both syncretic and tolerant when it comes to religion. In other words, they have created their own unique system of beliefs that borrows bits and pieces of theological perspective from a

> AMERICANS HAVE CREATED THEIR OWN UNIQUE SYSTEM OF BELIEFS THAT BORROWS BITS AND PIECES OF THEOLOGICAL PERSPECTIVE FROM A VARIETY OF FAITH GROUPS. CONSEQUENTLY, THEY ARE COMFORTABLE LETTING ANYONE BELIEVE PRETTY MUCH WHATEVER THEY WANT TO BELIEVE.

variety of faith groups. Consequently, they are comfortable letting anyone believe pretty much whatever they want to believe. This creative theological approach and open-mindedness is fueled by the collapse of moral truth in the past century and by the concurrent rise of the notion that faith is an optional supplement to one's life rather than its foundation. In this mind-set, every faith group is legitimate and everyone's truth is just as valid as everyone else's.

Thus, virtually every faith group is seen as adding value to the mosaic of American society. Half or more of all single adults have positive feelings toward each of the major religious groups in the nation, with the exception of atheists (if you can even consider them to be a faith group). Keep in mind, too, that most people have no idea what other faith groups believe or stand for, so their dominant impressions of almost every faith group besides the one to which they belong are based on either the few people they know who represent that group or how the media has portrayed that group.

While anywhere between one-seventh to one-third of singles do not know enough about any given faith group to have an impression of it, when those who do have an opinion pass judgment, it is generally positive. Among those with an opinion, 88 percent of singles have a favorable impression of Jews, 87 percent have a positive feeling about Catholics, and 81 percent have a positive outlook on evangelical Christians. Somewhat fewer singles—71 percent—have a positive opinion toward Muslims in the U.S. (this percentage may have changed since the September 11 attack on America). The exception to the pattern of positive thinking relates to atheists. While Americans have become more comfortable with atheism over the years, a majority of people with an opinion on atheists (and that constitutes 4 out of 5 singles) lean toward the negative end of the spectrum—only 44 percent have a favorable impression of atheists.

TABLE 5.1

SINGLES' OPINIONS OF MAJOR FAITH GROUPS

(View of those with an opinion)

	No Opinion	Favorable	Unfavorable
Evangelical Christians	23%	81%	19%
Jews	19	88	12
Catholics	14	87	13
Muslim Americans	30	71	29
Atheists	18	44	56

Source: A nationwide telephone survey by the Pew Research Center, September 2000.

For the sake of context, the opinions of married adults closely resemble those of unmarried adults. The primary difference is that married adults have even less favorable opinions of atheists.

AM I CHRISTIAN?

Most single adults think of themselves as Christian, although their depth of commitment to the Christian faith varies considerably. Eight out of 10 never-been-marrieds (78 percent) say they are Christian, which is slightly less than the 85 percent of divorced adults and 91 percent of widowed people. Very few singles claim to be atheists (10 percent of never-been-marrieds, 6 percent of divorced adults and only 4 percent of widowed adults).[1]

The tepid alignment of the never-been-married niche with Christianity is complemented by a generally weak commitment to the Christian faith. When singles who claimed to be adherents of the Christian faith were asked to describe how committed they are to Christianity, only 1 out of 3 never-been-marrieds (34 percent) said they were "absolutely committed." In comparison, half of divorced people who are self-described Christians (50 percent) said their commitment is absolute, and two-thirds of widowed Christians (68 percent) made the same affirmation.[2]

Why are never-been-married people so lukewarm toward Christianity? There is no simple or single reason for this. Among the chief reasons is the generational spiritual drift that is occurring these days, in which young adults use spiritual language and symbols to develop a unique and positive persona instead of embracing the deeper meaning that such symbols have traditionally reflected. Another important reason is the acceptance of the postmodern philosophy that suggests there is no right or wrong and that no particular faith has a corner on truth or righteousness, in addition to the belief that all faiths are of equal value. This thinking has reduced the intensity of allegiance that young people have to a specific faith, be it Christianity, Islam or Judaism. Add to this a generation-wide skepticism toward organizations, and we have the makings of a population group who will lead

America into the future without much sense of spiritual heritage or loyalty.

As the life stage of never-been-marrieds shifts from unmarried to married, a small portion of the group will alter its thinking and move to a more traditional perspective on faith alignment and commitment. But with each passing generation, we see a continued erosion of the depth of commitment to the Christian faith in America. We have no reason to believe that this pattern will suddenly change for the better.

WHAT PILLARS OF FAITH MATTER TO ME?

Single adults have developed an idiosyncratic view of what is important in one's faith emphasis. Examining the Early Church, as described in Acts of the Apostles, it appears that the foundations of the Church are sixfold: worship, evangelism, personal spiritual development, resource stewardship, community service and fellowship. These are the pillars of the Christian faith and constitute the dimensions of faith practice and development that form the basis of healthy Christians and churches. Yet, our research related to these pillars suggests that most churches and believers treat this list as a menu to choose from rather than an integrated set of foci that cannot be broken into isolated components. Americans, whether single or married, tend to identify one or two pillars with which they feel comfortable, and then they focus upon developing themselves in those areas, resulting in incomplete and unbalanced believers. Churches fall prey to the same miscue, producing specialty, or "boutique," churches that emphasize one or two pillars and pay lip service to the others.[3]

As we study singles' reactions to the importance of eight different faith-related emphases, we find that they generally have developed a discernible sense of the relative significance of each of these faith dimensions.[4] Worship is easily perceived to be the most significant of these undertakings, as three-quarters of all single adults described worshiping God as very important. Learning about the content of one's faith trailed, with two-thirds labeling that activity as very important. Experiencing true spiritual and moral accountability and serving the needs of the poor were embraced by slightly more than half of all singles. About 4 out of 10 unmarried people lumped sharing your faith with others, feeling like you belong to a faith group and meeting with other people of your faith as highly significant tasks. Lowest on the list was material stewardship, cited by only one-third as very important.[5]

TABLE 5.2

THE IMPORTANCE OF DIFFERENT FAITH EMPHASES

(Percent who said "very important")

Faith Emphasis	SGL	NBM	WID	DIV	MAR
Worshiping God	74%	70%	85%	75%	78%
Learning about the content of your faith	64	61	76	63	62
Experiencing moral and spiritual accountability	57	52	73	58	61
Serving the poor	56	50	73	54	55
Sharing your faith with others	42	37	65	39	44
Feeling like you belong to a faith group	38	33	48	38	44
Meeting with other people of your faith	38	34	53	35	39
Donating time and money to ministry	35	31	47	36	43

Key: SGL=all single adults; NBM=never-been-married; WID=widowed; DIV=divorced; MAR=married.
Source: A nationwide telephone survey by the Barna Research Group, November 2000. The study randomly surveyed 1,002 adults, including 479 singles.

There are substantial distinctions in the views that each singles niche has of each focus. In considering all eight of these emphases, we can see that never-been-marrieds are the least excited about them (their average "very important" rating across the eight emphases was 46 percent), while divorced adults (average score of 50 percent) and their married counterparts (average score of 53 percent) are slightly more convinced of the importance of these endeavors. Widowed adults are by far most persuaded of the significance of these matters, with two-thirds of the group (65 percent on average) citing each factor as "very important."

To assess the relative importance of each of these emphases in the eyes of the different singles segments, table 5.3 provides an index for each of the factors. This analysis indicates that compared to all adults, never-been-marrieds do not have a single spiritual emphasis among the pillars that reached the national average. In other words, representatives of that singles niche are more complacent about all of these efforts than are other Americans. Learning the content of their faith is their "hot button"—what is most important—but even that is lukewarm. Emphases such as donating time and money to ministry and feeling like you belong to a faith group are the least compelling elements in their minds.

Widowed adults are at the opposite end of the spectrum. Their levels of enthusiasm for each of the eight elements tested surpassed that of every other singles niche as well as that of married people. In relative terms, they seem most attracted to sharing their faith, serving others in need and meeting with other people of their faith.

Divorced adults fall somewhere in between the youngest and oldest singles niches on seven of the eight dimensions. That may give us insight into the fact that age plays a significant part in determining the importance people assign to these endeavors. Since most divorced people are between their mid-30s and mid-50s, the "averageness" of their response may be as much a generational response as a personal, spiritual reflection.

TABLE 5.3

AN INDEX OF THE IMPORTANCE OF DIFFERENT FAITH EMPHASES

(100=national adult average)

Faith Emphasis	SGL	NBM	WID	DIV	MAR
Worshiping God	99	93	113	100	104
Learning about the content of your faith	102	97	121	100	98
Having real moral and spiritual accountability	97	88	124	98	103
Serving the poor	104	93	135	100	102
Sharing your faith with others	95	84	148	89	100
Feeling like you belong to a faith group	93	80	117	93	107
Meeting with other people of your faith	97	87	136	90	100
Donating time and money to ministry	90	79	121	92	110

Key: SGL=all single adults; NBM=never-been-married; WID=widowed; DIV=divorced; MAR=married.
Source: A nationwide telephone survey by the Barna Research Group, November 2000. The study randomly surveyed 1,002 adults, including 479 singles.

Overall, divorced adults are relatively lukewarm on these areas of spiritual focus, failing to exceed the national average on any of the eight emphases. The four aspects that seem least compelling to divorced people are evangelism, feeling like they belong, spending time with others in their faith group and donating time and money to ministry.

> SINGLE ADULTS, IN ESSENCE, ARE SEARCHING FOR A CHURCH THAT WILL PROVIDE THEM WITH COMFORT, FRIENDS AND SOME GOOD INFORMATION.

Single adults, in essence, are searching for a church that will provide them with comfort, friends and some good information. There is shockingly little interest in pursuing real spiritual depth. One out of 5 single adults said that what they want most from a church is to feel good or happy as a result of their engagement with the ministry. Another one-fifth said they're seeking friends, and 1 out of every 6 wants to know more about what the Bible says. (Divorced and widowed adults were nearly twice as likely as never-been-married singles to list Bible knowledge as a desirable product of their church participation.) Relatively few individuals are seeking any type of specific personal spiritual growth. An alarming one-quarter of the churched singles interviewed admitted that they had no idea what they want from their involvement with church.[6]

AM I EXPERIENCING SPIRITUAL GROWTH?

Discussing the meaning of spiritual growth with Americans is an interesting challenge. It became quite clear during our research that few adults—whether married or single, male or female, young or old, black or white or Hispanic, highly educated or illiterate, Protestant or Catholic—spend much time thinking about why or how they should grow spiritually. Most Americans are satisfied to go through the motions of their habitual spiritual practices, blindly assuming that repetition of those actions will please God and build up their self-esteem.

Most single adults state that they are on top of spiritual growth. Two-thirds of the never-been-married and three-fourths of the divorced and widowed segments say they devote some of their personal time to growing or developing spiritually. There are, however, two distinct types of individuals who consider themselves to be Christian and engage in intentional spiritual development activity: those who pursue depth on a regular basis and those who never or only rarely do so. There were very few individuals in between the extremes. Among all self-described Christian singles, 2 out of 5 (41 percent) tend to engage in spiritual development practices during a typical week, 1 out of 10 (11 percent) do so at least once a month but less often than weekly, and the other half do so even less frequently, if at all.

Spiritual development is a two-sided coin—one side relates to intelligently pursuing growth, and the other side relates to evaluating and redirecting that growth. Currently, only half of all self-professed Christian singles say their church has helped them to think through and identify specific, reasonable and measurable goals for spiritual growth. Even fewer single adults—just one-third of the never-been-married group and two-fifths of the remaining singles—say they have standards they use to help evaluate their personal spiritual vitality. In other words, most singles who consider themselves to be Christian and are at least tangentially involved in church life have almost no way of determining whether or not they are growing spiritually, whether or not they are making progress and generally how spiritually mature they are.

A deeper examination of spiritual growth standards, which are relied upon by only a minority of singles, reveals that their substance is not very helpful. The standards typically concern how many times they attend church or how many times they read the Bible. These are not bad things to measure, of course, but neither do they tell us much about the development of the person's mind, soul and spirit. More than 4 out of 5 single adults lack any significant measures of their relationship with

Christ, their commitment to practicing different, Spirit-led ways of life or more consistent engagement with God in a deeply personal way.

In one national survey, we asked people to describe what it means to grow spiritually. Their answers were quite revealing. Most single people gave us two or more ideas about the meaning of spiritual growth. However, the vast majority talked about general things that they might do. Very few singles described what growth actually is or what types of life changes or personal outcomes they were seeking. Most often we heard about events and activities, rather than the outcomes that they were pursuing or specific evidence of positive spiritual development.

The most frequent responses dealt with common behaviors—reading the Bible, praying and attending church more regularly. A majority of single adults provided at least one of these activity-based answers. About 3 out of 10 single adults listed some type of lifestyle change or evidence of spiritual depth, such as helping other people, demonstrating kindness or generosity, or being a better or more godly individual. Some people—roughly 1 out of every 5—alluded to simply focusing on spiritual growth through discussion or seeking more information. About 1 of 10 single adults admitted they had no idea what the concept "spiritual growth" means.

TABLE 5.4

WHAT "SPIRITUAL GROWTH" MEANS TO SINGLES

Meaning of Personal Spiritual Growth	SGL	NBM	WID	DIV	MAR
To read or study the Bible	36%	38%	27%	41%	43%
To pray or have quiet times with God	33	39	25	31	35
To get more involved in church	16	18	10	19	17
To help others/volunteer	15	11	27	13	15
To show the fruit of the Spirit in my life	14	14	10	13	11
To interact with others about spirituality	13	10	14	16	14
To be a good or godly person	13	14	19	6	13
To gain more religious knowledge	12	9	15	14	15
Don't know what it means	9	10	6	9	12

Key: SGL=all single adults; NBM=never-been-married; WID=widowed; DIV=divorced; MAR=married.
Source: A nationwide telephone survey by the Barna Research Group, May 2000. The study randomly surveyed 1,003 adults, including 458 singles.

One of the most disturbing revelations was the response to a question about openness to their church involving them in a more intensive discipling process. When asked how they would react to leaders in their church helping them to identify specific procedures and ways to pursue a more mature faith, one-third (36 percent) of all self-proclaimed Christians who attend church said they would welcome such advice and assistance; half said they would listen to some of the ideas offered but would determine on their own what, if anything, to follow; and the remainder said they would either ignore the advice or leave the church.

> WHEN SPIRITUAL LEADERS CHALLENGE PEOPLE TO GET MORE SERIOUS ABOUT THEIR FAITH IN CHRIST, MASSIVE NUMBERS OF CHURCHED PEOPLE EITHER TURN A DEAF EAR OR TURN AROUND AND WALK OUT THE DOOR, NEVER TO RETURN.

We have found consistently that when spiritual leaders challenge people to get more serious about their faith in Christ, massive numbers of churched people either turn a deaf ear or turn around and walk out the door, never to return. Helping believers to grow by introducing specific steps of life or providing accountability for efforts to achieve such outcomes are not popular ideas.

The most damning evidence of all, however, has to do with the identity of churched singles in regard to what they consider to be the most desirable outcomes of spiritual growth efforts. For most singles, the

most desirable outcomes are self-focused, suggesting that a large number of self-described Christians who are single perceive spirituality to
be anchored on the self rather than God. Roughly half of all singles
describe the desired outcomes of spiritual investment to be emotional
security (e.g., feeling good about myself, feeling at peace with the world
or feeling happy), better relationships with other people (e.g., feeling
more connected with others, having better friends or feeling like I'm part
of a group of people who understand me) and generic personal improve-
ment (e.g., being a better person or improving my skills). The other half
listed more plausible outcomes such as having a better relationship with
God, knowing more content of the Bible, engaging in the spiritual disci-
plines and having a meaningful personal ministry to other people. (One
out of every 4 adults mixed the self-focused and God-focused outcomes
into a very Americanized hybrid.) One-quarter of all self-described Christian singles said they have no idea what they want to achieve in terms of
personal spiritual growth.

In essence, when singles who align themselves with the Christian
faith think about where they are going with that faith, the group is
divided into quadrants. One-quarter are completely selfish, thinking
only about how they can use faith to attain their worldly goals. One-
quarter are focused solely on deepening their experience with God.
One-quarter are juggling worldly and otherworldly objectives, striving
to keep both ends in harmony. And one-quarter don't give spiritual
growth a second thought; they simply go through some religious routines until they achieve greater clarity about their life's meaning.

WHAT ARE MY SPIRITUAL GIFTS?

How sophisticated is the spiritual knowledge and commitment of singles? One measure suggests that the superficiality alluded to through
the previously discussed measures is accurate. When we quizzed singles who describe themselves as Christian about spiritual gifts, we discovered that about 7 out of 10 had heard of spiritual gifts. Of those,
just 6 out of 10 never-been-marrieds and divorced adults and 8 out of
10 widowed adults claimed to possess a spiritual gift. Upon asking

people to identify those gifts, the level of ignorance and misinformation was astounding.

A closer look at the data provides three important insights. First, even among the relatively few single adults who have heard of spiritual gifts, a large percentage do not know what their gifts are. Second, the older the people are, the more likely they are to claim specific gifts, suggesting that many young people and young adults waltz through their first two or three decades of life ignorant of who they are and how God has prepared them to serve—potentially hindering, not only their impact for His kingdom, but also their sense of value in God's eye and their uniqueness in His creation. Third, and most disheartening of all, half of all single adults identified "spiritual gifts" that are not the special abilities described in the Bible. Among the spiritual gifts claimed by singles were patience, good health, having children, musical ability, a nice apartment, dancing, tolerance and a fine radio!

TABLE 5.5

THE SPIRITUAL GIFTS CLAIMED BY SINGLE ADULTS

(Base: single adults who consider themselves to be
Christian, say they have heard of spiritual gifts and
believe God has given them one or more gifts)

Type of Spiritual Gifts Mentioned	SGL	NBM	DIV	MAR
Leadership-related gifts	6%	9%	5%	9%
Communication-related gifts	13	9	20	17
Revelation-related gifts	19	14	23	13
Outreach-related gifts	8	6	14	18
Service-related gifts	10	8	11	20
Nonbiblical gifts	47	49	52	48
Have gifts but don't know what they are	19	18	14	10

Key: SGL=all single adults; NBM=never-been-married; DIV=divorced; MAR=married.
Definitions: Leadership-related=apostle, administrator, leader, shepherd and pastor; communication-related=encouragement, exhortation and teaching; revelation-related=discernment, interpretation, knowledge, prophecy, tongues and wisdom; outreach-related=evangelism, healing, hospitality, intercession and mercy; service-related=giving and helping.
Source: This is based on a nationwide telephone survey by the Barna Research Group, May 2000. The study randomly surveyed 1,003 adults, including 458 singles.

In total, 12 percent of all singles listed only biblical spiritual gifts, 14 percent solely listed nonbiblical gifts, 2 percent listed a combination of biblical and nonbiblical gifts, and 6 out of 10 single adults had no idea about gifts (either because they do not label themselves as Christians, they have never heard of gifts, or they believe God has not given them gifts).[7]

Imagine what could happen if single adults were better informed about how God has entrusted a special gift or combination of gifts to each of His followers. The informed application of those people's gifts in life and ministry could radically change the self-perception, the spiritual fervor and the Kingdom impact of tens of millions of unmarried people. We ought not to wait until these people are in their 20s, 30s or 40s to broach the topic. Teaching young believers about their gifts and helping them find ways to hone and use those special abilities as they age would create an incredible impact in their lives and the world in which they serve.

But the present condition, which is that most single adults are clueless about gifts, is indicative of a much deeper and more serious problem: the spiritual complacency and ignorance of single adults. Knowing about spiritual gifts is of little value to a person who does not see him- or herself as created to love God through personal purity, worship and devotion to God, and to serve others.

FATUOUS FAITH

Consider this: Fewer than 5 out of every 100 single adults in America are absolutely committed to the Christian faith, are actively seeking to grow in each of the pillar areas of spirituality, regularly invest themselves in intentional spiritual growth efforts and can identify and give evidence of using their spiritual gifts to serve God and His people. The percentage of never-been-married singles that fit this description represents only half the number found among widowed and divorced adults. In every singles niche we studied, the percentage is in the single digits. Clearly, there is much growth yet to be accomplished!

CHAPTER 6

THE RELIGIOUS PRACTICES OF SINGLES

A few years ago, the phrase "Show me the money!" from the movie *Jerry Maguire*, spoken by a pro football player to his ever-promising, never-delivering agent, captured the imagination of the American people and became part of the daily lexicon. The public related to the player's fatigue with unfulfilled albeit good intentions; he simply wanted his agent to make good on his promises.

In the same way, we might imagine God observing all the posturing about religiosity and listening to the omnipresent talk about spirituality in America, pursing His lips, shaking His head and bellowing from on high, "Show me the faith!"

Jesus harshly criticized those who played the religious game but failed to live the spiritual life. For Him, the proof is in the practice. Talking about faith is not nearly as crucial as living the faith. How deeply have single adults invested themselves in actions that might bear spiritual fruit?

For younger singles, involvement is a more unique commitment, since fewer of them grew up in families that regularly involved them in spiritual endeavors. Fewer than 6 out of 10 (57 percent) never-been-married adults regularly attended a Christian church when they were growing up, compared to 3 out of 4 divorced adults and 8 out of 10 widowed adults.[1] Given our recent research, which shows the dramatic effect on adult's religious behavior attributable to attending church when young, the lack of religious routines and experiences among the never-been-marrieds puts them at a distinct spiritual disadvantage.

RELATING WITH A CHURCH

In a typical week, slightly more than 1 out of every 3 single adults attend a church service. Presence at a church service is much more likely among widowed adults (half are present on an average weekend) than among divorced people (slightly more than one-third) or never-been-married adults (not quite 3 out of 10). The oft-heard complaint of single adults— church is for married couples and families—may well be attributed to the fact that married people and their children are more likely to show up at church than are singles. Fifty-one percent of married adults attend a church service in a typical week, which is nearly 50 percent higher than the number of singles appearing in the pews. Add to that the reality that married adults bring more people with them and that they donate greater sums of money and hours of volunteer labor, and the alleged bias of churches toward families is more understandable, although not justifiable.[2]

Single adults cannot make the argument that their unique lifestyle simply makes them too busy or too committed to other responsibilities to enable them to attend church. In a survey conducted between six and eight weeks after the terrorist attacks in 2001, church attendance had declined somewhat from the unnaturally high levels of the first two weeks after the attacks but was still slightly above the norm. Four out of 10 never-been-marrieds, 6 out of 10 widowed folks and slightly more than 4 out of 10 divorced adults attended church. (The portion of married adults attending was little changed, clocking in at 55 percent, which is only a few percentage points higher than the preattack average.)[3]

> # THE CHURCHES THAT SINGLE ADULTS HAVE CHOSEN TO ASSOCIATE WITH ARE SOMEWHAT DIFFERENT FROM THOSE THAT ATTRACT MARRIED ADULTS.

Additionally, the churches that single adults have chosen to associate with are somewhat different from those that attract married adults. About one-fifth of singles and married folks attend Baptist churches. One-quarter of married people associate with mainline Protestant congregations, compared with just one-eighth of never-been-marrieds, one-fifth of the divorced and nearly one-third of the widowed. (Put differently, widowed singles are more than twice as likely as the younger, never-been-married singles to align with mainline churches.) Never-been-marrieds are the most likely singles niche to attend a Catholic church (28 percent compared with 19 percent of widowed, 22 percent of divorced adults and 26 percent of married adults). Comparatively few single adults—1 out of 20—attend nondenominational churches, although the portion that does so is identical to that of married adults.[4]

Surprisingly, single adults are more likely than married adults to attend a small church. Most unexpected of all is that divorced adults are the most likely singles segment to attend a church with fewer than 100 adults in average attendance. Only 1 out of 10 single adults goes to a megachurch, compared with 1 out of 8 married people. A key reason for the attraction of larger churches among married people is the presence of a larger and assumedly better-quality children's ministry. Given the paucity of significant singles ministries among smaller churches, one might imagine that single adults are not as likely to view church as a place to meet a potential mate as was the case a couple of decades ago.[5]

PARTICIPATING IN WEEKLY RELIGIOUS ACTIVITY

It is important to make a distinction between the quantity of religious activities undertaken and the quality or impact of those experiences. If we focus on the amount of religious activity that occurs in the lives of single adults, the sheer volume of time and energy devoted to religious involvement is enormous—not as widespread as would be desired, of course, but substantial nevertheless.

The only religious activity of the 8 measured in table 6.1 in which a majority are involved in a typical week is praying to God, an act that 4 out of 5 single adults claim to engage in. Half of all singles have a quiet time or private devotional time during the average week. Only one-third of the unmarried population attends church services during a typical week, and the same portion reads from the Bible at times other than while at church. Fewer than 1 out of 5 single adults volunteers at church, attends a Sunday School class or participates in a small group or cell group during an average week. Singles are 50 percent more likely to volunteer their services to a nonprofit or charitable group during a typical week than they are to offer themselves to the ministry of their church.

Each singles segment experienced different levels of activity and relative involvement. The never-been-married group was the least likely of the 3 major subgroups to be engaged in spiritual activities. In fact, this segment was the least likely to participate in 6 of the 8 efforts measured and was tied for the lowest involvement in the other 2. There was only one activity that at least half of the never-been-married folks engaged in—prayer—and just one other endeavor that attracted more than one-third of them in a typical week—having a personal quiet time. Even though devotional times were the second-highest rated activity among this group, they were the only subgroup studied among whom less than half were so inclined. Never-been-marrieds were nearly twice as likely to volunteer at a nonprofit organization or charity as they were to help at a church. And despite their relatively young age and their interest in finding a soul mate, just 1 out of 7 from this niche involved themselves in a small group. Given their alleged interest in spirituality and relationships, this percentage—again, the lowest mark among the four segments studied—is surprising but underscores the overemphasis analysts have placed on the spiritual commitment of young adults.

TABLE 6.1

THE RELIGIOUS PRACTICES OF AMERICANS
IN A TYPICAL WEEK

Religious Activity in Past Seven Days	SGL	NBM	WID	DIV	MAR
Read from the Bible, other than at church	36%	29%	52%	39%	42%
Attended a church service, other than special event	35	29	49	37	51
Volunteered to help at a church	18	14	28	20	29
Volunteered free time to help a nonprofit organization, other than a church or synagogue	27	24	28	30	32
Prayed to God	80	74	90	85	84
Attended a Sunday School class	15	13	24	14	23
Participated in a small group, other than a Sunday School class or 12-step group, that meets regularly for Bible study, prayer or Christian fellowship	15	14	22	15	21
Spent some quiet time by yourself reading the Bible or devotional literature and praying, other than while you were at church	50	40	72	57	54

Key: SGL=all single adults; NBM=never-been-married; WID=widowed; DIV=divorced; MAR=married.
Source: National telephone surveys by the Barna Research Group, January 2000-July 2001. The study randomly surveyed 3,148 married adults and 2,847 single adults.

Widowed adults had the most active involvement in a range of religious pursuits. In fact, they ranked highest among the three singles niches on all 8 of the endeavors tracked. They were more likely than married adults to engage in 3 of the 8 activities and equally likely to engage in the other 5. More than half of all widowed people read the Bible, attend church, pray and have a private devotional time during an average week. They are twice as likely as other singles to attend a Sunday School class, almost two-thirds more likely to have a personal devotional time and about 60 percent more likely to read the Bible than are other singles.

Divorced adults held the middle ground on 5 of the 8 items when compared with never-been-married and widowed singles. The only 2 religious actions that more than half of divorced adults engage in during a typical week are praying to God and having a personal devotional time. Overall, divorced people are somewhat skeptical about deeper involvement in church life because of their assumptions regarding how the congregation will respond to their marital status.

Compared to married adults, singles are less likely to be involved in each of the 8 activities assessed. The biggest gaps were in endeavors such as church attendance (a 16-point differential), church volunteerism (an 11-point gap) and Sunday School attendance (an 8-point distinction).

Many social analysts suggested that the terrorist attacks on America in 2001 changed the spiritual tenor and fervor of the nation. Our research showed that not to be the case. Based on a national study conducted two months after the terrorist attacks, we found that the religious practices of Americans, including singles, had barely changed. Immediately after the attacks, a huge surge occurred in church attendance. The postattack attendance was recorded at 9 percentage points above the preattack level for singles. The percentage of singles attending church reached 44 percent. Prayer, Sunday School attendance, volunteerism, small group involvement and devotional times all remained static. The number of single adults who volunteered their time at a church continued to trail the number who volunteered their time to other nonprofit and charitable organizations (29 percent). Within each of the segments, never-been-marrieds were the only group to increase their church volunteer efforts (jumping from 14 percent to 21 percent—a small aggregate but a 50 percent increase from the preattack level). Never-been-marrieds' involvement in small groups also rose by 6 percent. Widowed people exhibited a substantial decrease in quiet times, dropping from 72 percent to 61 percent. Divorced people showed the greatest rise in Bible reading (up 6 percent) and Sunday School attendance (up 11 percent). For the most part, however, the levels of activity remained surprisingly consistent after the attack.[6]

Least Popular Religious Activities

Among the activities we measure on a monthly basis are financial support (since people's paychecks arrive at different intervals and thus affect giving patterns). We found that within a typical month, slightly less than half of all singles donate some money to a church. The usual pattern is evident across the three primary singles segments: Widowed adults are most likely to donate (66 percent), then divorced people (50 percent), distantly followed by the never-been-marrieds (34 percent). For context, realize that two-thirds of married adults (64 percent) donate money to a church during an average month.[7]

We also learned that singles are nearly as likely to give money to other nonprofit organizations, besides churches, as they are to support a community of faith. Nearly 4 out of 10 singles (37 percent) gave to other nonprofits and charities in a typical month. Again, widowed people lead the way (52 percent give to such causes), followed by divorced people (45 percent) and the never-been-marrieds (29 percent). Half of all married adults give to nonchurch organizations during a typical month.

Consider the following four insights related to giving. First, most never-been-marrieds do not give to any organization. Second, both divorced and never-been-married people are nearly as likely to give to nonchurch entities as to a church. Third, despite their limited incomes and the less likelihood of seeing their income rise, widowed people are the most generous singles. Finally, comparing these figures to similar data from a decade earlier, church giving has decreased. In 1991, never-been-married and divorced singles were more likely to donate to a church than they are today. For the most part, we are examining the behavior of a different group of people than those who fit these marital states a decade ago. In addition, the ways in which these individuals relate to churches regarding their giving has changed significantly over time.

The amounts of money donated to churches and nonprofits over the course of a year also vary considerably. The mean amount given to churches in the calendar year 2000 ranged from just $239 among the never-been-married segment to $412 among the divorced, $570 among the widowed and $1023 among married people. In related fashion, we found that two-thirds of never-been-marrieds donated something to a church, three-quarters of the widowed followed suit and 4 out of 5 divorced adults displayed some generosity. All three segments, however, were shown up by married adults—85 percent donated to a church in 2000. Among those who give anything to a church, most of their giving winds up in church coffers. About 59 percent of the money donated by never-been-marrieds went to churches, compared with 71 percent of the money donated by widowed people and 80 percent of the funds contributed by divorced adults. Married people barely led the pack, giving 81 percent of their total donations to churches.

We also tracked people's engagement in evangelism. Generally speaking, single adults are just as likely as married people to share their faith in Christ with a nonbeliever during the year. Slightly fewer than 6 out of 10 born-again adults, whether single or married, had done so during the past year. Breaking the established pattern, the group most likely to have shared their faith was the never-been-married contingent. (Keep in mind, however, that this is based upon a subset of each singles population—those who are born-again Christians.)[8]

Finally, we explored the act of holding a leadership position in a church. Married adults were about 50 percent more likely to hold such posts than were single adults. Among the singles, just 1 out of 8 was involved in such an act of service, most often in a teaching capacity. The differences among the singles niches were huge. Only 7 percent of the never-been-married group held a leadership position, compared with 11 percent of the divorced and 29 percent of the widowed. Keep in mind that these figures do not reflect people's willingness to serve in a leadership position but whether or not they were invited to do so by their church and then agreed to fill the position.

UNDERSTANDING THE UNCHURCHED

About 3 out of 10 single adults are unchurched, which means they have not attended a Christian church service other than a holiday service or a special event (such as a wedding or funeral) within the past six months. The subgroups within the singles population who are most likely to abstain from church attendance are men, singles who do not have a college degree, residents in the Northeast and the West, and Protestants.

Half of the unchurched singles in our nation are unable to recall the name of even one church located within 15 minutes of their home. Combined with the revelation that most unchurched singles have never been invited by a churched person to attend a church service, we can posit that church life is not on the minds of most unchurched singles.

The research also shows that we often misunderstand how unchurched people want to be treated should they choose, for whatever reason, to visit a church. Most unchurched people want to be left alone when they visit, except for receiving a genuine greeting from church regulars either before or after the service, a thank-you note from the pastor during the week following their attendance and the opportunity to pick up some background information about the church without any sales pitch or other pressure accompanying the information. They do not want to be singled out for special attention, they don't want special gifts, and they don't want to explain their presence at the church by publicly declaring why they're visiting or who brought them. They want to come, check out the people and develop a visceral response to an emotional experience rather than a mental response to an intellectual experience.

THE FUTURE CHURCH: GOING ONLINE

As technology becomes an increasingly ingrained aspect of American life, you can expect a growing number of people to turn to the Internet for spiritual experiences and expression. By the end of this decade, close to 1 out of every 10 Americans will have completely rejected the bricks-and-mortar church in favor of a cyberchurch experience. This movement is generational more than familial in character. We can already see that this mind-set is affecting ministry, particularly among those who today are in the never-been-married category (many of whom will be in the divorced category a decade from now).

Currently, most single adults contend that they are more likely to have a superior spiritual experience, regardless of what spiritual dynamic is studied (e.g., worship, discipleship, service or stewardship) through a physical church rather than through a cyberchurch. The aspects of spirituality for which the Internet is likely to be deemed a better vehicle than the physical church include evangelism and Christian education, but even for these areas barely 1 out of 8 singles would argue that the Internet is more conducive to a positive experience than a physical church. That is one reason why few singles say they are likely to abandon a physical church completely and replace it with a cyberchurch.

However, people have a terrible track record of predicting personal change. We believe that the acceptance of the cyberchurch will be just one more example of people not foreseeing future shifts in behavior. Most people will not make that shift during our lifetime, but a substantial number of single (and married) adults are already engaged in the process of making this transition.

A key example of this change of emphasis is evident in singles' likelihood, even during this early era in the nascent history of the cyberchurch, to use the Internet to satisfy each of a number of spiritual needs. As you examine the figures in table 6.2, you will see a substantial openness toward, and expectation of, using the Internet to help them fulfill their spiritual quest.

Half of all adults, single and married, expect whenever the mood strikes to use the Internet to access religious teaching archived on a website by listening to it via audio-streaming technology. Not surprisingly, never-been-married adults, who are more technology savvy than their older single counterparts, are the segment most likely to engage in such activity.

About 9 out of every 20 single adults currently plan to use the Internet to submit prayer requests and to access short religious readings that will motivate, focus or challenge themselves.

Four out of 10 singles, led by the never-been-married group, expect to use the Internet to purchase books and study guides regarding religion and matters of faith.

One out of 3 single people (37 percent) plan to use the Internet to engage in an online independent study course that focuses on faith matters. A similar portion expects to use the Internet as the medium through which they will purchase Christian or religious music in the near future.

Three out of 10 unmarried adults say they will use the Internet to participate in an online chat room or discussion group that focuses on religious matters, to engage in a real-time online Bible study group, to participate in an online class that meets regularly to study some particular aspect of religion or faith and to gain coaching in spirituality by a more mature believer. In each of these dimensions, the never-been-married group is most enthusiastic, while the older singles display muted anticipation.

The least enthralling spiritual possibility to singles is the prospect of real-time worship experienced online via a video-streaming process. Only 17 percent of all singles expressed interest in this potential ministry avenue.

When all of these ways in which adults expect to use the Internet are combined, we find that more than 4 out of 5 single adults have some aspect of faith or spirituality in mind for which they expect the Internet to be useful. As the years pass and the Internet becomes established as a standard component in our daily experience, and as technology evolves to facilitate a higher-quality online religious experience, these figures will steadily rise. The cyberchurch will grow slowly but consistently as people become accustomed to online experiences related to faith, as other dimensions of our life make digital experiences a more common and socially acceptable substitute for more traditional experiences and as the technology improves.

TABLE 6.2

Ways in Which Adults Expect to
Use the Internet to Meet Their Spiritual Needs

Way in Which They Could Use the Internet	SGL	NBM	WID	DIV	MAR
To listen to religious teaching contained in archives of teachings that you could access whenever you want, on whatever topic is of interest to you	51%	54%	41%	46%	50%
Submit prayer requests to a group that prays for people's needs	45	48	36	41	35
Read a short religious reading to motivate, challenge or focus you	44	49	31	42	45
Buy books or study guides about religion or faith	41	45	27	41	42
Participate in an online, independent study course related to faith matters	37	41	28	33	32
Buy religious music	34	38	24	28	30
Participate in a chat room or online discussion group regarding religion or faith	31	36	21	25	21
Participate in a Bible study that takes place online, in real time	30	33	25	25	27
Participate in an online class that meets regularly to study some aspect of faith or religion	30	33	23	27	29
Be mentored or coached in spiritual development by a person whose faith is more developed than yours	29	29	21	28	22
Worship God through a real-time, video-streaming worship experience	17	17	11	18	13

Key: SGL=all single adults; NBM=never-been-married; WID=widowed; DIV=divorced; MAR=married.
Source: This is based on a national survey by the Barna Research Group, November 2000. The study randomly surveyed 1,003 adults, including 479 single adults. For a more extensive exploration of the role of the Internet in people's faith life, consult a research report entitled *The Cyberchurch* (Ventura, CA: Barna Institute, 2001).

Investing in the Spirit

There are two levels on which we might assess the spiritual involvement of single adults. On the absolute level, in which we consider people's personal spiritual investments in comparison with biblical standards, we

WE FIND THAT MORE THAN
4 OUT OF 5 SINGLE ADULTS
HAVE SOME ASPECT OF FAITH
OR SPIRITUALITY IN MIND FOR
WHICH THEY EXPECT THE
INTERNET TO BE USEFUL.

would have to conclude that relatively few Americans, married or not, are intensely committed to being true disciples of Christ. On a less stringent level, in which we compare singles to married adults, we must note that the higher levels of spiritual investment by married folks certify that a deeper level of involvement is feasible. Clearly, single adults lack a compelling motivation to abandon the world and devote themselves to the things of God. Finding those hot buttons that will encourage single adults to reorient their priorities and invest in their spirituality is, as the apostle Paul would say, "a worthy goal" (see Phil. 4:12-14).

CHAPTER 7

WHAT SINGLE
ADULTS BELIEVE

What we believe about God, truth and faith matters—a lot. Understanding people's beliefs is critical to influencing them, because these are the bases on which they develop their core values. Those values, in turn, direct personal behavior.

Despite claims that we live in a Christian nation, the fact that more than 4 out of 5 Americans consider themselves to be Christian or the evidence that more than 85 percent of the places of worship in America are dedicated to the pursuit of the Christian faith, we cannot afford to fall for such superficial diagnoses of the nation's spiritual condition. America is no more a Christian nation than China is a democracy. True, we have elements of Christian heritage, there are millions of dedicated Christians in the country, and we are relatively comfortable with Christian symbols and language. But in the place where it really counts—

our hearts—we are far removed from the type of Christian faith, experience and lifestyle that Jesus spoke of during His brief ministry on Earth.

BELIEFS ABOUT THE BIBLE

Like other citizens, most single adults—9 out of 10 of them—own a Bible. However, the first red flag we encounter relates to the version of the Bible most of them rely upon for insight into God's Word—the *King James Version* (*KJV*). Although married adults are slightly more likely than singles to use the *KJV* as their primary version, about one-third of singles use this 400-year-old translation. Four times as many single adults use the *KJV* as use the next most popular version—the *New International Version* (*NIV*). There is nothing inappropriate about owning and using a *KJV* Bible, except for the fact that most Americans do not possess the literacy skills to interpret adequately the language used in the *KJV*. One must wonder what would happen if more single adults were introduced to more contemporary, reader-friendly translations of the Bible.

We can reasonably expect that a more accessible Bible version would increase singles' reading of the Bible and maybe even their enjoyment, appreciation and comprehension of its content. Currently, just 1 out of 8 single adults reads the Bible on a daily basis; 1 in 5 reads it less than daily but at least weekly; 2 out of 4 read it infrequently; and 3 out of 10 never read it.

Perhaps a different version of the Scriptures would influence what single adults believe about the Bible itself. Presently, one-quarter contends that the Bible is the actual Word of God, to be taken literally, word for word. A similar portion argues that the Bible is the inspired Word of God, containing no errors but including some symbolism. One out of 6 says that the Bible is the inspired Word of God that contains some historical and factual errors. Fewer single adults believe that it is not an inspired book but a collection of views held by the authors of each book (1 out of 10) or that it is a book of teachings from men in the form of stories or advice (1 out of 8). Surprisingly, this profile differs little from that of married adults.

Indisputably, the best argument for transitioning millions of single adults to a more reader-friendly version of the Bible is to clarify what they think the Bible teaches. Most singles have a head full of theological notions. One must wonder, though, about the source of such musings, for it certainly is not the Bible.

Biblical Accuracy

In addition to whether single adults think the Bible is inerrant or inspired, the research shows that a slim majority of single adults (53 percent) believe that the Bible is accurate in all that it teaches. However, it is also important to note that only a minority of singles—just one-third—strongly affirm the accuracy of the Bible's teachings, ranging from 31 percent of never-been-marrieds to 41 percent of the divorced to 46 percent of the widowed.[1] People within the singles niches most likely to

> ONLY A MINORITY OF SINGLES—JUST ONE-THIRD—STRONGLY AFFIRM THE ACCURACY OF THE BIBLE'S TEACHINGS.

believe in the accuracy of Bible content are women (41 percent strongly affirm the Bible's accuracy compared to just 30 percent of single men), blacks (57 percent firmly argue that Scriptural teaching is accurate, nearly double the 32 percent of white singles who think similarly) and people who do not have a college degree (40 percent strongly agree with this idea compared with just 30 percent of the singles who have a college degree). Protestant singles are twice as likely as Catholic singles to affirm strongly the complete accuracy of the Bible's teachings (51 percent versus 25 percent, respectively).

One of the most common distortions of biblical teaching is the notion that the Bible literally contains the principle that God helps those who help themselves. The three-fourths of married folk who agree with this idea are not alone in their erroneous thinking. The same portion of single adults buys into this view. In fact, a majority of single adults (55 percent) strongly agree that this is a notion found in the Bible. For unknown reasons, this idea is more widely accepted by divorced adults (67 percent strongly believe the perspective is stated in Scripture) than by widowed (52 percent) or never-been-married people (48 percent).

BELIEFS ABOUT SIN, FORGIVENESS, SALVATION AND EVANGELISM

Singles embrace a mixed bag of beliefs related to sin and salvation. To their credit, most believe that sin is still a relevant concept for our day. Only 1 out of every 14 single adults strongly argues that sin is an outdated concept. At the other end of the spectrum, 6 out of 10 single adults strongly affirm that sin is present today. Although young singles are the least likely to accept the concept of sin, a majority firmly defends its significance for understanding modern life.

Few single adults are aware of, or even understand, the contradiction between saying that there is no absolute moral truth on which to base daily choices and that sin exists. Therefore, is sin a relative reality? That is, is sin for me not necessarily sin for you? Our research on this matter clearly demonstrates that few people have thought about the relationship of sin, goodness, truth and salvation. In fact, as postmodernism becomes a more entrenched philosophy in America, people are becoming more comfortable with such contradictions and feel less of a need to reconcile views that cannot logically coexist.

Despite accepting the reality of sin, many single adults also embrace the mistaken notion that all people will experience the same outcome after they die, regardless of whether they accepted Jesus Christ as their Savior or not. Four out of 10 singles believe this notion. Twice as many never-been-marrieds concur, while only one-third of the widowed and two-fifths of the divorced concur. A slightly higher portion of single adults—half—disagree that everyone will have the same eternal outcome.

The appeal of such optimistic thinking relates to the widespread notion that all faiths teach the same lessons, which eliminates the distinctiveness of any particular faith and makes acceptance of a faith group more significant than the identity and unique attributes of the group with which you associate. A slightly higher portion of single adults (half) accept the idea that all of the world's major religions teach the same basic lessons, while about 4 out of 10 unmarried Americans reject that notion. Young singles are the least likely to reject this notion—just 1 out of 4 singles under 35 strongly disagrees that all faiths teach the same core truths.

These ideas result in tainted beliefs about the possibility of, and means to, eternal salvation. Fifty-five percent of all single adults agree that if a person is basically good or does enough good things for other people, he or she will earn a way into heaven. Only 1 out of 4 single adults firmly disagrees that good deeds are the route to salvation. This belief also illuminates a critical misunderstanding among most Americans, that is, people are inherently good. Scripture informs us that once sin invaded our hearts, we ceased to be pure and now sin is endemic to all human beings. Jesus did not have to die a cruel, unjust, humiliating and painful death on a cross because we are good people but because we are wicked, perverse, sinful beings at heart. Only through spiritual rebirth that comes from accepting Christ as our Savior and inviting the Holy Spirit to control our lives does the potential for goodness take on any significant meaning in our lives.

Four out of 5 single adults believe that God has given people free will and that it, in turn, enables people to choose their eternal destiny. Six out of 10 singles feel quite strongly about this freedom to choose; it fits snuggly into the American mold of self-determinism and the desire to have control and multiple options from which to make such choices.

Regarding salvation, most Americans, married or not, claim to have made a personal commitment to Jesus Christ that is still important in their lives today. Six out of 10 single adults make such a claim, as do half of all never-been-marrieds and 7 out of 10 widowed and divorced adults. This is a curious claim in light of other admissions by the same people, such as the fact that many do not describe themselves as absolutely committed to the Christian faith or that they do not view their religious faith as very important in their lives today.

When those who claim such a personal commitment to Christ are asked about life after death, we find that making a personal commitment to Jesus and trusting Him for salvation are two different matters. Among the 6 out of 10 who say they are committed to Christ, only 57 percent say that they are certain they will go to heaven after they die solely because they have confessed their sins and have accepted Jesus as their Savior.

In essence, that means only one-third of single adults (35 percent) have become born-again; that is, they no longer trust in their own good deeds as a means to reconciliation with God but rely completely upon God's grace through Christ's death and resurrection. Never-been-married adults are the least likely to meet the born-again criteria—only 29 percent qualify. Higher percentages of widowed (44 percent) and divorced (42 percent) adults are born-again, but there are still more married adults (47 percent) who qualify as such.[2]

We have also discovered that Hispanic singles are less likely to be born-again (22 percent) than are white (35 percent) or black (48 percent) singles. The two factors most responsible for this are the traditional Catholic background of most Hispanics (placing a substantial focus on personal effort as a means to earning God's favor, along with prayers to Mary and other saints) and their youthfulness (most Hispanics in America are under 40). Nationally, only 19 percent of Catholic singles are born-again, compared to 54 percent of Protestant singles. The age factor is also undeniable: Only 28 percent of singles under 35 are born-again, compared with 38 percent of those who are 35 to 49 years of age, 42 percent of those in the 50 to 64 age bracket and 44 percent of the 65 and older crowd.

Americans who claim commitment to Christ have all kinds of ideas regarding their eternal destiny. Among single adults who have made such a commitment, 17 percent admit that they do not know what will happen to them after they die. Ten percent say that they will be in heaven because they were basically good people on Earth. Smaller percentages of singles who claim to be committed to Christ say they will be in

TABLE 7.1

WHAT AMERICANS BELIEVE

Perspective	SGL	NBM	WID	DIV	MAR
The Bible is totally accurate in all of its teachings					
Agree strongly	37%	31%	46%	41%	45%
Agree somewhat	16	18	14	15	16
Disagree somewhat	22	24	19	21	19
Disagree strongly	19	22	11	17	15
Don't know	6	6	9	5	6
You personally have a responsibility to tell other people your religious beliefs					
Agree strongly	28	24	36	31	36
Agree somewhat	16	17	16	16	17
Disagree somewhat	23	25	22	21	19
Disagree strongly	30	33	22	31	27
Don't know	2	2	5	2	2
Your religious faith is very important in your life					
Agree strongly	64	56	79	70	72
Agree somewhat	19	22	13	17	15
Disagree somewhat	9	12	5	7	7
Disagree strongly	7	8	3	5	5
Don't know	1	2	1	1	1
The devil, or Satan, is not a living being but is simply a symbol of evil					
Agree strongly	41	39	44	43	37
Agree somewhat	20	23	15	16	18
Disagree somewhat	9	10	8	8	8
Disagree strongly	23	23	23	23	31
Don't know	7	6	10	9	7
If a person is generally good or does enough good things for others during life, he or she will earn a place in heaven					
Agree strongly	34	34	35	31	31
Agree somewhat	21	24	17	18	17
Disagree somewhat	12	12	11	14	11
Disagree strongly	25	23	27	28	34
Don't know	8	7	10	9	7
When He lived on Earth, Jesus Christ was human and committed sins like other people					
Agree strongly	25	27	20	25	22
Agree somewhat	21	24	16	18	18
Disagree somewhat	9	10	7	9	8
Disagree strongly	36	31	46	40	45
Don't know	9	8	12	8	8
Number of respondents	2,847	1,576	446	700	3,148

Continued on next page

TABLE 7.1—*Continued*

Key: SGL=all single adults; NBM=never-been-married; WID=widowed; DIV=divorced; MAR=married. *Source:* Eight national surveys by the Barna Research Group, January 2000-November 2001. The studies randomly surveyed 2,847 single adults and 3,148 married adults.

heaven because God loves all of the people He created and will not allow any of them to perish (7 percent) or because they have done a stellar job of obeying the Ten Commandments (5 percent). About 3 percent have other, idiosyncratic views.

> # JUST 1 PERCENT OF ALL SINGLES BELIEVE THAT THEY WILL GO TO HELL.

Here's the kicker—just 1 percent believe that they will go to hell. Americans will talk about sin, forgiveness, grace, salvation and the like; but most Americans cannot bring themselves to face the possibility that they might live their postflesh lives in a state of adversity with the God of all creation.

As for the connection between salvation and evangelism, there is some good news and some bad news. The bad news is that most single adults are not relying upon Christ for their salvation. The good news is that most singles do not feel they have a responsibility to share their religious beliefs with individuals who see things differently from themselves. Only 3 out of 10 singles strongly believe that they have a duty to share their faith with others, and most of these people are born-again Christians. So why is this good? Because 4 out of 10 singles who embrace the responsibility to share their spiritual beliefs are not born-again, which could muddy the waters, since most likely they are sharing a faith that is not based solely on the Bible. If you hope to motivate believers to share the truths of Christ with others, the singles most likely to get excited about the challenge are women, blacks and people 50 or older. Single adults under the age of 35 are especially reluctant to proselytize to their friends, because tolerance, diversity and postmodernism have labeled efforts to influence people's thinking about faith a cultural no-no.

BELIEFS ABOUT THE TRINITY AND THE ADVERSARY

Two out of 3 single adults have an orthodox, biblical view of God. Given a set of 6 possible views of God, the most popular choice is the description of God as an "all-powerful, all-knowing, perfect creator of the universe who still rules the world today." Six out of 10 never-been-married adults adopt this view, compared with 7 out of 10 other single and married adults. Other views of God are less prolific. Eleven percent claim that "God signifies a state of higher consciousness that a person may reach." One out of 12 singles (8 percent) suggest that "God refers to the total realization of all human potential." Four percent say that everyone is God; 3 percent believe that "there are many gods, each with different power and authority"; and 3 percent say there is no such thing as God. Five percent don't know what to think.

These statistics indicate that nearly 3 out of 10 single adults embrace a New Age perspective on the nature of God. Most of those who reject a biblical perspective of God perceive deity to be a state of personal development rather than the existence of a holy being with dominion over humanity. Single males are more likely than single females to embrace such a view (27 percent versus 22 percent, respectively), and singles under 35 are more likely than their older unmarried peers to buy into such a concept (27 percent). Black singles were the least likely to embrace the New Age view (14 percent). Amazingly, 1 out of every 12 born-again singles has a New Age portrait of "God" in mind.

Oddly and despite these statistics, 7 out of 10 single adults strongly agree that God created the universe, and 85 percent agree either strongly or somewhat strongly in the creation. This is odd because less than that percentage believe in God as an omnipotent creator. Perhaps a slice of the unmarried population accepts the view that God created the world but is no longer involved in it—a notion popular in some circles—which would be appealing to some singles, given their overall spiritual perspective.

One out of 3 singles is willing to limit God's power by suggesting that there are some sins that not even God Himself can forgive. In fact, only half of the singles niches believe strongly that this view is incorrect, which provides further evidence that Americans are relatively confused about God and His purposes, power and plans.

> WHILE MOST SINGLES CONTEND THAT JESUS WAS A REAL HISTORICAL FIGURE, HALF ALSO CONTEND THAT HE COMMITTED SINS WHILE HE WAS ON EARTH.

Even fuzzier thinking prevails when it comes to the reality of Jesus Christ. While most singles contend that Jesus was a real historical figure, half also contend that He committed sins while He was on Earth. This view is much more common among young singles and those who have never been married than among older singles and those who have some marriage experience. Black singles are the least likely to reject the holiness of the Son of God by asserting that He sinned; only 38 percent of them buy into this view, compared with 47 percent of white singles and 53 percent of Hispanic singles. Unmarried people living in the Northeast are also particularly prone to this view (53 percent). Amazingly, 30 percent of born-again singles believe that Jesus sinned.

In like manner, more than 4 out of 10 single people (43 percent) say that Jesus died but never had a physical resurrection, as claimed in the Bible. Some would submit that perhaps He had a spiritual resurrection but not a bodily return from the dead after three days.

The perceived existence of Jesus is placed in context by the fact that only half of the never-been-married segment, two-thirds of the widowed contingent and 7 out of 10 divorced people strongly affirm that Jesus Christ is alive today. While fewer than 1 out of 10 singles believe strongly that He is not alive, a large portion falls in the gray zone of leaning one way or the other, which implies that they do not have a firm stance on the matter.

Singles' views on other supernatural beings appear no less confusing. For instance, more than 4 out of 10 singles strongly agree that the Holy Spirit is not a living being but is simply a symbol of God's power or presence. In fact, two-thirds of all singles maintain some level of agreement with this idea. Only 1 out of every 5 singles strongly denies that the Holy Spirit is merely symbolic. Astoundingly, born-again singles are no different from their unsaved counterparts with respect to the opinion that the Holy Spirit does not exist.

Americans, including most single adults, generally dismiss the existence of Satan. Four out of 10 single adults strongly agree that Satan is merely a symbol of evil rather than a living being, and 2 out of 3 singles agree to some extent with that view. Fewer than 1 out of 4 single adults firmly resist the idea that Satan is symbolic. Once again, shockingly little difference exists between the views of single Christians and those of single non-Christians on this matter.

THE BIBLE BELT LIVES ON

One of the enduring cultural realities of the U.S. is the existence of the Bible Belt. Although virtually everything related to traditional spiritual practices and institutions has taken a beating in the past half century—and the Bible Belt has not escaped the influence of paganism and postmodernism—the Southern states remain notably different in spiritual climate and practice. Single adults in the South are becoming more like the typical adult throughout the nation but at a slower rate of change. Generally, people in the Northeast and West have moved the furthest from biblical views, people in the South are the most likely to hold biblical views, and folks in the Midwest sit somewhere in between the extremes.

TABLE 7.2

What Single Adults Believe, by Region

Perspective	NE	SOU	MW	WST
Religious faith they consider themselves to be				
Christian	76%	88%	84%	77%
Non-Christian faith	10	5	6	9
Atheist/agnostic	10	4	7	12
The Bible is totally accurate in all of its teachings				
Agree strongly	29	47	36	31
Disagree strongly	23	13	18	23
You personally have a responsibility to tell other people your religious beliefs				
Agree strongly	20	37	29	24
Disagree strongly	37	21	30	37
Your religious faith is very important in your life				
Agree strongly	57	73	62	59
Disagree strongly	9	4	5	9
The devil, or Satan, is not a living being but is simply a symbol of evil				
Agree strongly	44	43	40	38
Disagree strongly	20	25	20	26
If a person is generally good or does enough good things for others during their life, they will earn a place in heaven				
Agree strongly	38	31	31	35
Disagree strongly	20	29	25	23
When He lived on Earth, Jesus Christ was human and committed sins like other people				
Agree strongly	27	24	24	25
Disagree strongly	30	41	39	32
God is the all-powerful, all-knowing creator of the universe who still rules the world today	60	74	65	57
Born-again Christian (made personal commitment to Christ that's still important, and believe they will go to heaven because they confessed their sins and accepted Christ as their Savior)	23	46	36	30

Key: NE=Northeast; SOU=South; MW=Midwest; WST=West.
Source: Seven national surveys by the Barna Research Group, January 2000-November 2001. The study randomly surveyed 2,847 single adults and 3,148 married adults.

As is evident in table 7.2, single adults in the Northeast and West are the least likely to describe themselves as Christian, to assert strongly that the Bible is accurate, to contend firmly that they have a personal responsibility to evangelize, to reject the notion that Jesus sinned, to possess a biblical understanding of God's nature, to claim that their faith is very important to them and to fit the born-again criteria. They are the most likely to affirm strongly that a good person can earn eternal salvation.

On the other hand, single adults living in the South remain the most likely to describe themselves as Christian, to assert strongly that the Bible is accurate, to contend firmly that they have a personal responsibility to evangelize, to describe their faith as very important in their life, to reject the notion that Jesus sinned, to maintain a biblical understanding of God's nature and to meet the survey definition of "born-again." Southern singles are the most likely to dismiss the notion that a good person can earn eternal salvation.

Over the next few decades, the regional distinctions that we see today are likely to disappear. One major reason is the mobility of our population. With 1 out of every 6 households changing location each year and young adults demonstrating an even higher rate of mobility than was evident in the past, there will be a heightened mixing of backgrounds. Add to that the homogenization of the nation's churches, the virtual absence of spiritual training within the family unit and the increasing impact of the mass media upon people's spiritual inclinations, and we have great reason to expect the elimination of regional differences in the not-too-distant future.

CHAPTER 8

ARE CHRISTIAN SINGLES DIFFERENT FROM OTHERS?

Christianity is not meant to be merely a series of religious exercises that change our schedules but not our hearts. The Christian faith is meant to be life transforming, causing us to be more like Jesus Christ. Such change should be evident in every dimension of our lives—emotional, interpersonal, intellectual, financial, vocational and recreational, as well as spiritual. In God's economy, no room exists for shallow faith. We either devote ourselves to His way of life or sell out to the world's way, and there is no place in between where the complacent or weak may hide. Yet this transformation is a lifelong process that will never be complete until those who embrace Jesus Christ as their Lord and Savior are reunited with Him in heaven. We are called to be obedient but not expected to be perfect.

How are unmarried Christians doing in this spiritually driven life transformation? It's not an easy factor to assess. One means of evaluating the state of the Christian singles population is to compare their standing on a variety of factors with that of single nonbelievers. Throughout this chapter, as I have in this entire book, I will be defining "Christian" singles as those who meet the "born-again" criteria we use in our surveys, which means that they say they have made a personal commitment to Jesus Christ that is still important in their life today and believe they will have eternal life with God in heaven only because they have confessed their sins and accepted Christ as their Savior.

LIVING LIKE A BELIEVER

The most overt and definitive way to discern an individual's commitment to Christ is by observing the manner in which he or she lives. Many dimensions comprise our daily experience, and each is susceptible to change once we choose to imitate the life and values of Jesus. Let's briefly explore how Christian singles view themselves regarding seven areas of self-perception.

Life Purpose

While Christian singles are slightly less likely to describe themselves as "too busy" (40 percent do so, versus 47 percent of non-Christian singles), they are no less likely to describe themselves as "stressed-out." One-third of single adults who have accepted Christ admit that they feel overwhelmed by anxieties and pressures. Part of this feeling of helplessness is undoubtedly related to the fact that about half of all single adults, regardless of their faith commitment, say that they are still searching for the meaning and purpose of their life. The absence of such insight invariably produces unnecessary and confounding stress on a regular basis.

It is curious that Christians would continue to struggle with the meaning and purpose of their life. There are two ways in which people might address this issue: (1) identifying their mission (i.e., the general purpose of being alive) and (2) identifying God's vision for their life (i.e., a specific and compelling mental portrait of a preferable future that God has called them to pursue).

> ONE-THIRD OF SINGLE ADULTS WHO HAVE ACCEPTED CHRIST ADMIT THAT THEY FEEL OVERWHELMED BY ANXIETIES AND PRESSURES.

Understanding mission is the first and easiest step, since it is the most general and generic. All believers are called to the same mission, which may be communicated in various ways but essentially relates to obeying Luke 10:27:

> "Love the Lord your God with all your heart and with all your soul and with all your strength and with all your mind"; and, "Love your neighbor as yourself."

Describing mission in terms that the individual resonates with is important, but possessing an understanding of what mission is and how it alone can direct one's life is a necessary and elementary step for believers. It appears that few believers have a grasp of the nature and significance of declaring their life's mission.

Vision conveys a deeper understanding of our uniqueness in Christ and His special expectation and calling to us. As our research into the process of understanding and implementing God's vision has shown us, this is something that takes greater time, effort, study and commitment.[1] However, vision is also one of the character traits of individuals who ultimately make great inroads for the Kingdom in their own sphere of life. Enabling people to distinguish between their personal vision (human driven) and God's vision (Spirit and Bible driven) is important in the maturation and clarification process.

The fact that half of all believers say they are searching for meaning and purpose suggests that they have yet to understand God's mission for their life. This is a shortcoming that we, as friends or leaders whom they trust, can help them overcome.

Career and Finances

Surprisingly few singles say that their career comes first in their life, and Christian singles are no more (or less) likely than others to make such a claim. Christians singles are, however, notably less likely than non-Christian singles to indicate that they like to try new experiences (70 percent versus 85 percent, respectively). While most singles like trying new things, fewer Christians appear to possess the adventurous spirit of nonbelievers.

One of the great pressure points in the lives of singles relates to finances. Christian singles were indistinguishable from their non-Christian counterparts in regard to finances, which may also help explain the identical stress levels of both segments. Our research shows that single adults are equally likely to say that they are struggling financially, in debt and living comfortably, regardless of their spiritual orientation and commitments.

Relationships

The personal relationships of believers also look very similar in some ways to those of nonbelievers. Although they are slightly more likely to describe themselves as "very relational," Christian singles are every bit as likely as nonbelievers to be actively searching for a few good friends, to engage in similar types of conversations with others and to prefer being in control of situations they encounter. Believers are more likely to try to avoid conflict with others and are less likely to be willing to make tough decisions. These two related perspectives suggest that many Christians may inadvertently disqualify themselves from leadership positions because they are more likely to shy away from the challenging situations that test and define leaders.

In addition to appreciating control, most singles, regardless of their faith orientation, see themselves as self-sufficient and tend to behave accordingly. No difference exists between the two segments in terms of their concern about the future, although the September 11 terrorist attacks did raise the level of concern among the non-Christians a bit more.

Sociopolitical Ideology

One of the biggest differences between the two groups relates to sociopolitical ideology. Christians are more likely to view themselves as mostly conservative (33 percent) than mostly liberal (10 percent), while non-Christian singles are slightly more likely to see themselves as liberal than conservative. Keep in mind, however, that the majority of all singles see themselves as being somewhere in the middle. Half of all Christian singles and 6 out of 10 non-Christian singles say they are "somewhere in between" the ends of the ideological spectrum. Born-again singles are also more likely to be registered to vote, more likely to be Republican, less likely to be Independent and more likely to have voted for George Bush than Al Gore in the hotly contested 2000 presidential election. Born-again singles gave Bush a small margin over Gore; non-Christian singles, on the other hand, supported Gore by a 2-to-1 margin.

Spirituality

The area of self-image in which believers and nonbelievers differ the most relates to spirituality. Six out of 10 non-born-again singles say they are "spiritual," compared to 9 out of 10 born-again singles. When we tightened the self-definition a bit and asked if they see themselves as "deeply spiritual," the numbers shrank accordingly—8 out of 10 believers embraced the label compared to only half of the nonbelievers.

One of the more intriguing outcomes was discovering that only two-thirds of the singles who fit the survey classification of "born-again" actually use that term to describe themselves. At the same time, one-fifth of those who do not meet the survey criteria for being born-again think of themselves as born-again Christians. Although only God truly knows who is and is not a disciple of Jesus, these research-based estimates suggest that we have to be careful about labels and stereotypes—even those that people adopt for themselves. Single adults who consider themselves to be born-again may not have the type of relationship with Christ that does, in fact, incorporate them into the true Church, while a single who does not use such a description may nevertheless have exactly the type of faith and life commitment that honors the Lord and thus qualifies them for such an esteemed title.

Music

Even beyond self-image, though, the research shows that single adults have other similarities and differences from peers who do not share their faith orientation. One such dimension is in the area of music. While all singles, regardless of spiritual leanings, are equally likely to purchase recordings throughout the year, the two groups prefer divergent types of music.

The three most widely appreciated musical styles of born-again singles are Christian, R&B and country, each named by more than 10 percent as their favorite genres. The least appreciated styles are country, rock and rap/hip-hop, each mentioned by at least 10 percent as their least-favored genres. When we compare the percentage of singles who like a genre and subtract the percentage of those who dislike the genre, a different picture emerges, one that portrays the types of music that people are most comfortable hearing. Those styles are Christian, R&B, pop, jazz and alternative (primarily among unmarried singles).

The profile is somewhat different among non-Christian singles. The preferred styles are rock and country. The most disliked styles are rap/hip-hop, country and rock. In other words, there is substantial heterogeneity among non-Christian singles. The net preference list includes R&B, jazz, pop, Christian and alternative.

One of the most significant insights this analysis brings to the table, though, is how splintered the singles market looks in terms of musical preferences. Because music is the single most powerful language in our culture today, it is important to provide people the sound with which they resonate. Doing so makes the statement that the ministry is sensitive to and in touch with the needs and desires of the target audience.

But clearly, the sound that attracts one group of singles may repulse another group. While R&B and Christian may be the "safest" sounds to employ in a ministry setting, they are also styles that will fail to move a large portion of the unmarried masses.

TABLE 8.1

MUSICAL PREFERENCES OF SINGLE ADULTS, BY FAITH ORIENTATION

Musical Style	Born-Again Singles			Not Born-Again Singles		
	Favorite	Dislike	Net Acceptance Points	Favorite	Dislike	Net Acceptance Points
Christian	24%	1%	+23	4%	2%	+2
R&B	14	*	+14	8	1	+7
Pop	6	1	+5	6	3	+3
Jazz	6	2	+4	6	1	+5
Alternative/grunge	4	*	+4	2	*	+2
Country	12	17	-5	11	18	-7
Heavy metal	*	8	-8	*	9	-9
Rock	9	20	-11	19	11	+8
Rap/hip-hop	3	33	-30	7	35	-28

* Indicates less than half of 1 percent.

Source: A national survey by the Barna Research Group, October 2000. The study randomly surveyed 1,017 adults.

Technology

One of the significant determinants of people's lifestyle (i.e., the use of technology) is generally similar between singles who are believers and those who are not. Levels of ownership of electronic equipment were virtually identical, and the ways in which the two niches use the Internet differed only slightly. Christian singles were somewhat more likely to use the Internet for faith-related experiences and for video games and somewhat less likely to keep up existing relationships through e-mail and online discussions. Overall, electronics are owned and used just as often—and deployed for the same reasons and in the same ways—by singles, no matter where they stand with Jesus Christ.

Thinking like a Believer

The goals that singles have set for themselves are flavored significantly by their religious inklings. There are certain life outcomes that both segments share an interest in experiencing, such as good health, clarity of life purpose and living with integrity. However, there are some huge gaps between the groups.

Priorities

Christian singles were more likely to prioritize having a close personal relationship with God (ranked first among the 21 possible alternatives, compared to a ninth-place finish among non-Christian singles), being deeply committed to the Christian faith (rated fifth by Christians and fifteenth by non-Christians) and being active in a local church (rated eighth by single Christians and nineteenth by nonbelievers). Notice that the dimensions that Christians rated more highly dealt with faith.

Non-Christian singles were much more likely to prioritize close friendships (their second-ranked goal, which was ranked sixth by believers), a comfortable lifestyle (third highest, compared with a tenth-place finish among believers) and a satisfying sex life with their marriage partner (seventh on their list but just thirteenth among believers). These factors relate back to comfort and security, which the Christian singles often expect to receive to a greater degree through their faith commitments.

Morals

The area in which faith leanings makes the greatest difference relates to moral perspectives. Christian singles have significantly different views from non-Christian singles in relation to 15 of the 20 areas of moral and ethical living that we studied. In fact, there are 12 areas in which the moral views of the two niches differ by more than 20 percentage points, which is the level at which those differences become practically significant rather than just statistically significant. The information shows that Christian singles are most likely to have different moral standards on issues such as abortion, homosexuality, cohabitation, sexual infidelity, pornography and drunkenness.

Also worth noting are some moral issues on which Christian singles have a divergent perspective from that of non-Christian singles, yet less than half of Christian singles maintain a conservative view on the matters. For instance, only 4 out of 10 Christians contend that there are moral absolutes, which is higher than the 3 out of 10 among non-Christians but still a relatively low percentage. The idea in Matthew 5:31-32 that divorce is a sin unless it is a response to marital infidelity is accepted by only one-third of Christian singles, which is twice the percentage of nonbelievers but still comparatively depressed. In like manner, it is disturbing to note that only half of Christian singles consider cohabitation to be morally unacceptable and sexual fantasies to be inappropriate.

TABLE 8.2

DIFFERENCES IN MORAL PERSPECTIVES OF SINGLES, BY THEIR FAITH COMMITMENT

Moral Perspective	Born-Again	Not Born-Again
There are moral absolutes that are unchanging	43%	29%
Abortion should be illegal in all or most circumstances	63	38
Homosexuality should be legal between consenting adults	42	65
Approve of clergy performing/blessing gay marriages	19	46
Except when related to adultery, divorce is a sin	35	18
Cohabitation is morally acceptable	47	79
Marijuana use for nonmedicinal purposes is morally acceptable	10	39
Having sexual relations with a person of same sex is morally acceptable	10	42
Watching a movie with explicit sex or nudity is morally acceptable	34	66
Reading a magazine with explicit sexual pictures or nudity is morally acceptable	26	65
Using profanity is morally acceptable	28	52
Getting drunk is morally acceptable	22	50
Having an abortion is morally acceptable	23	53
Speeding is morally acceptable	35	48
Having sexual thoughts or fantasies is morally acceptable	48	76

Source: A national survey by the Barna Research Group, May 2001. The study randomly surveyed 1,003 adults, including 491 single adults.

Christian singles also have some areas of moral and ethical perspective in which they are indistinguishable from their non-Christian peers. Among those are elements such as the basis of their moral decision making. Although you might expect Christian singles to rely more heavily upon influences such as the Bible or religious teaching, we found that this was not the case. Other dimensions of moral behavior on which the thoughts of Christian and non-Christian singles matched included having an affair with an unmarried person, keeping excess change knowingly received by mistake and lying on a resume to increase one's chances of securing a desirable job.

TABLE 8.3

MORAL PERSPECTIVES THAT ARE SIMILAR AMONG BOTH CHRISTIAN AND NON-CHRISTIAN SINGLES

Moral Perspective	Born-Again	Not Born-Again
The basis of your moral/ethical decisions is		
The Bible	17%	12%
Values taught by your parents	13	12
Whatever feels right or comfortable in the situation	24	26
Whatever produces the best personal outcome	13	14
Having an affair with an unmarried person is morally acceptable	21	28
Keeping excess change given to you by mistake is morally acceptable	15	19
Lying on a resume about your education or job achievements is morally acceptable	10	11

Source: A national survey by the Barna Research Group, October 2000. The study randomly surveyed 1,017 adults.

BELIEVING LIKE A BELIEVER

Just as believers and nonbelievers have different views on many moral issues, so do they possess a variety of divergent theological perspectives. Keep in mind that one of the key theological differences relates to whether or not they are born-again (only 1 out of every 3 singles is born-again). Also remember that just 1 out of every 7 born-again singles is an Evangelical, meaning that they are not only born-again, but they also believe that the Bible is accurate, that they have a responsibility to share their faith with nonbelievers, that Satan is real, that Jesus was holy, that salvation cannot be earned and that God is the holy, omnipotent and omniscient creator and ruler of all things. The fact that so few people who trust Christ for their salvation believe these core biblical truths is a revealing commentary on the state of the Church today—and on the lack of spiritual depth among single adults.

From a macrolevel vantage point, note that most people, whether they know Jesus intimately or not, think of themselves as Christian. Three out of 4 non-Christian singles use that label. Also, most of today's single adults were churched while growing up—83 percent of the born-again singles and 57 percent of the non-born-again singles were churchgoers when they were young—which is something that will change with the emerging generations (i.e., the Mosaics). Little that occurs in church will surprise most singles, and a large share of them (more than three-quarters) think they already know all the core beliefs of the Christian faith and therefore have little to learn.

The specific beliefs of the two segments diverge, however, on most theological matters that go beyond simplistic concepts. Christians are three times more likely to contend strongly that the Bible is accurate in its teachings, to assert that they have a duty to share their faith and to deny strongly that a good person can earn salvation. Christians are twice as likely as nonbelievers to describe themselves as "absolutely committed" to Christianity, and to believe firmly that God created the universe and that Jesus is alive today. They are twice as likely as nonbelievers to deny strongly that all of the major faith groups teach the same lessons that Jesus never had a physical resurrection, that Jesus committed sins, that Satan is symbolic but not real and that the Holy Spirit is symbolic but not real. Believers were also notably more likely to assert that their faith is very important in their life and that God gives us free will that allows us to choose our eternal destiny. They are also much more likely to reject the idea that there are some sins that God cannot forgive. Even on a simple matter such as perceptions of God's nature, born-again singles were very different. Nine out of 10 born-again singles endorsed the view of God as the all-knowing, all-powerful creator, while only half of the nonbelievers accept this view.

While the single adults who follow Christ are notably different from other singles in their religious views, it is important to recognize that there is ample room for growth in their theological maturity. For instance, only one-third of Christian singles strongly reject the idea that Satan doesn't exist but is merely symbolic. Less than half of all believers firmly believe that salvation cannot be earned—an amazing statistic given that all of these individuals are personally relying on grace rather than good deeds as their means to eternal security. Less than one-third strongly disagree that the Holy Spirit does not exist, which produces some devastating theological consequences. Barely half of all single believers strongly deny that Jesus ever had a physical resurrection, again raising serious questions about either the biblical knowledge or the depth of confidence in Scripture that these people possess.

TABLE 8.4

WHAT CHRISTIAN AND NON-CHRISTIAN SINGLES BELIEVE

Perspective	Born-Again	Not Born-Again
The Bible is totally accurate in all of its teachings		
Agree strongly	62%	23%
Disagree strongly	5	26
You personally have a responsibility to tell other people your religious beliefs		
Agree strongly	49	17
Disagree strongly	12	40
Your religious faith is very important in your life		
Agree strongly	87	51
Disagree strongly	1	10
The devil, or Satan, is not a living being but is simply a symbol of evil		
Agree strongly	39	43
Disagree strongly	36	16
If a person is generally good or does enough good things for others during their life, they will earn a place in heaven		
Agree strongly	22	40
Disagree strongly	44	15

Continued on next page

TABLE 8.4—CONTINUED

Perspective	Born-Again	Not Born-Again
When He lived on Earth, Jesus Christ was human and committed sins like other people		
Agree strongly	18	29
Disagree strongly	58	24
The Holy Spirit is a symbol of God's presence or power but is not a living entity		
Agree strongly	46	43
Disagree strongly	31	12
God is the all-powerful, all-knowing creator of the universe who still rules the world today	89	52

Source: One or more national surveys by the Barna Research Group, January 2000-November 2001. Each study randomly surveyed 1,000-plus adults.

When we quizzed people about the importance of each of the eight key religious activities, nonbelievers were less likely to rate each of these as "very important" than were believers. While more than half of the believers described each of the eight endeavors as very important, only two of those practices reached that level of significance among nonbelievers (i.e., worshiping God and learning about their faith). Fellowship, stewardship, evangelism, serving the needy and accountability were all deemed to be of great importance to half or less than half of the non-Christian singles population.

Non-Christian singles are generally leery of getting too deeply involved or invested in personal spiritual development. Just one-third have standards they use to evaluate their spiritual condition—a statistic that was identical to that of Christian singles—and they are slightly less likely than believers to follow ideas provided by leaders and those who disciple, who would take them under their wing and strive to help them grow in Christ. This may be due to fear of the unknown. When nonbelievers were asked to describe their content of personal spiritual growth, they were three times more likely than believers to say they had no idea what that might entail or the product they would seek for growth.

ARE CHRISTIAN SINGLES DIFFERENT?

Clearly, Christian singles are in a different place spiritually and morally than are nonbelievers, which is good for the Church. This provides the Church with a contingent of disciples who can reasonably be expected to share their faith with non-Christians and help those individuals mature in their faith.

> NON-CHRISTIAN SINGLES ARE GENERALLY LEERY OF GETTING TOO DEEPLY INVOLVED OR INVESTED IN PERSONAL SPIRITUAL DEVELOPMENT.

The statistics underscore the importance of using opportunities to interact with non-Christian single adults and being aware that they are coming from a different point of view on many aspects of life, ranging from values and morals to beliefs and relationships. Ministering to groups is difficult in this regard unless the group is truly homogeneous, which in turn suggests that perhaps we have not done an adequate job of reaching out to the majority who do not know Christ and who do not have much to do with the Church. If we are attracting single adults to activities at church, we have to remember that they view the world through a different set of lenses. We must tailor our interaction with them accordingly—never compromising the gospel and its implications—and must always contextualize those elements so that the uninitiated can understand what we are saying, embrace it and then follow it.

CHAPTER 9

MAKING THE MOST OF MINISTRY TO SINGLES

Now that the evidence has been presented, would you agree that there are very distinct singles populations that require special attention and unique interaction if we are to know, love and serve them appropriately? Whether you interact with single adults at work, in the neighborhood, through leisure pursuits, within your family or in a ministry context, addressing their individual needs, preferences, expectations and lifestyles, you must have an accurate knowledge of where they're coming from and where they're going. Like most Americans, single adults generally want to be known and loved, accepted for who they are and helped in areas in which they are weak. You and I have a tremendous opportunity to be agents of influence and transformation in the lives of unmarried people

if we adequately understand what makes them tick and what we can do
to facilitate their maturation.

> # LIKE MOST AMERICANS, SINGLE ADULTS GENERALLY WANT TO BE KNOWN AND LOVED, ACCEPTED FOR WHO THEY ARE AND HELPED IN AREAS IN WHICH THEY ARE WEAK.

Let me summarize some of the conclusions I've drawn from this
body of information. First, let's consider what we need to know about all
singles groups, and then we'll consider some of the idiosyncrasies of
each of the three major singles niches. You might have drawn entirely
different conclusions or developed different priorities based on the
information presented so far—and that's great! My motivation is to provide a summary interpretation and exhortation for you to ponder. The
bottom line, though, is for you to be so confident that you have something to offer to single adults, and to become so intentional and strategic in how you choose to reach out to those people, that you will act with
vigor, wisdom and faith. Nothing is worse than understanding without
action! No matter what conclusions you have drawn, commit yourself to
putting your insights and ideas into action.

WHAT ALL SINGLE ADULTS NEED

One of the striking realities about America's unmarried population is that
just one-third has accepted Jesus Christ as their Savior. Increasing that
percentage needs to be a priority for the Church—but what will it take?

Prayer

At the risk of sounding simplistic, single adults who do not know the saving love of Christ need our prayers. Can you become an intercessor for one single adult? Can you recruit other prayer partners to adopt other unsaved single adults and pray them toward the Cross? Focused, sincere prayer from godly people changes the world. You can become part of a moral and spiritual revolution by praying without ceasing for the souls of specific people. Find a single adult who is seeking to make it from day to day without Christ dwelling in his or her heart and pray him or her into the Kingdom!

If you are able to engage in a more interactive approach, consider how you might get singles truly to engage in God's Word. Singles are lukewarm toward the Bible. Their refusal to read it consistently, to take its content at face value and to translate its substance into a worldview based on truth has undermined their capacity to know and emulate Christ. Confounding the situation is their belief that they already know what the Bible has to say and their stated intention not to alter their views about what they think the Bible teaches. In reality, young singles remain largely ignorant of the Bible's principles, while older singles appear to be anesthetized to its truths.

Study the Bible

For some singles, a valuable first step would be to obtain a version of the Scriptures that they can more readily understand. Most unmarried adults need help in becoming reacquainted with the Bible through creative introductions to the content. They need to get beyond the basic stories they have heard since childhood and instead incorporate personally meaningful applications in their lives. All of this must be done purposefully, however, which demands study and teaching that leads to a coherent, comprehensive and compelling worldview. The last thing single adults need is a tidbit of truth here and an interesting idea there. For decades, they have had exposure to elements of truth without having the dots connected to display God's grand perspective. Although they cannot articulate the need, singles are desperately seeking the revelation of that grand design—not just the means to salvation, but the mosaic of wisdom that reveals God's greater purposes and interwoven truth. Until these things are shown to singles in clear and unmistakable ways, they will continue their fruitless, frustrated search for meaning, purpose and fulfillment in life.

> ## FOR SOME SINGLES, A VALUABLE FIRST STEP WOULD BE TO OBTAIN A VERSION OF THE SCRIPTURES THAT THEY CAN MORE READILY UNDERSTAND.

Walk

Once singles achieve an appreciation for the Bible and get a grip on God's unchanging truths, it will be possible for them to concentrate on deepening their spiritual maturity by intelligently and passionately focusing on the pillars of faith. While most singles have an area or two of faith that they truly embrace as significant, it is their lopsided, incomplete perspective on Christianity that enables their lukewarm following toward Christ to continue. Helping singles to understand the identity and significance of the pillars and to evaluate realistically where they stand in relation to the six focal points of the faith will constitute a major leap forward toward becoming stellar believers.[1]

Ultimately, of course, these new insights and perspectives should impact their values and resulting lifestyle choices. This is one benefit of having a godly worldview: It serves as the filter through which every decision is evaluated and every choice is made. Upon observing how single adults live—especially those who claim to be followers of Jesus—if the fruit in their lives does not support their claim to being a disciple, then those who serve the Church must hold these unmarried peers accountable for their choices and behaviors. This is true for never-been-married, divorced and widowed adults. The fact is that few singles have biblical standards and loving accountability integrated into their daily efforts and enforced by caring Christian peers.

Critical elements in our ability to help single adults grow, however, are our commitment to a genuine relationship with them and our ability to model an authentic Christian life. Like most people, singles shield themselves from the influence of those whom they do not know and trust. They are most open to ideas and constructive criticism from people with whom they have developed a true bond. Outsiders who engage in "hit-and-run discipleship"—that is, criticizing others without having first established credibility through relationship—often do more damage than benefit for the Kingdom through their well-intentioned but reckless approach. To gain serious consideration from singles, you need to show your real concern for who they are by taking the time and making the effort to engage them in true friendship.

At the same time, friends undermine the credibility of their words if their behavior does not demonstrate the truths they profess and the expectations they convey to others. Millions of Americans, single as well as married, distance themselves from the Church and the ways of Christ because of the overt hypocrisy of alleged believers. Few Americans—especially those who are likely to reject the existence of absolute morality and the purity of the Christian faith—winningly pursue a faith that seems inherently impossible to live or innately flawed on the basis of how it is portrayed by its followers. The individuals who make inroads for Christ in the lives of others are those believers who not only demonstrate the love of Christ by investing themselves in significant relationships but who also pursue and reflect the life principles of Jesus in their personal behavior.

WHAT NEVER-BEEN-MARRIEDS NEED

To impact the lives of those who have never ventured into marriage, keep in mind what turns their crank: satisfying relationships, group activities, interesting adventures, authenticity, efforts that build or reinforce their self-esteem, and opportunities to succeed. The more you are able to incorporate an understanding of these needs into your interactions with them, the more trusted and relied upon you will become and the greater your opportunity for influence.

Because these singles tend to be younger adults and are therefore still feeling their way through the process of becoming established in the workplace and within a network of supportive relationships, offering them options that educate while facilitating meaningful interaction will be welcomed. Taking the time truly to listen and to provide a process of discovery rather than a standard package of indisputable answers fits their needs. Using media, music and language that reflect their background and expectations is beneficial as you attempt to gain their attention and consideration. Resist establishing the goal of building "the biggest singles ministry in town." Instead, strive to create an environment in which they experience energy, value, acceptance, purpose and hope, in order to facilitate sincere involvement and significant personal growth.

Few never-been-marrieds have a significant understanding of the spiritual pillars of faith, although they would debate such a statement. It may seem simplistic, but you will need to introduce them to what it means to experience the presence of God in worship, how to develop and implement a biblical worldview, why personal brokenness and an urgency for forgiveness and holiness are needed and how to get there, what wholistic stewardship means and holding them accountable for practicing it, why serving the needy is imperative and how to get involved in such service, and how to develop biblical community. If this seems like an exercise in introducing basic Christian foundations, that's because it is; and it's precisely what they have missed out on all of their lives.

WHAT WIDOWED ADULTS NEED

Widowed adults live life at quite a different pace, and that's the way they prefer it to be. They have paid their dues and seen it all, and most widowed adults want to enjoy a peaceful existence during the years they have left. They do not want more responsibility, control or conflict. They are happy to help a ministry, but they don't want to shoulder its burdens.

They are more comfortable with predictable routines than exciting surprises. The ministry that understands this mind-set and strategically works within its boundaries will thrive.

Although most widowed adults are more spiritually mature and more interested in pursuing matters of faith than the average single adult, they do have points of vulnerability. They attend church services as their health allows, and they feel attendance is in itself a statement. But surprisingly few of them really understand the reality of experiencing God's presence and interacting with His Spirit in a personal and worshipful way. Helping them to gain a deeper understanding of worship will open up new vistas on life for the widowed.

A portion of the widowed population will respond to the opportunity to mentor a younger person, as long as it can be done in their own style. Don't expect written plans, extensive reading lists and rigorous assessments; they are more likely to recount some of the lessons they have learned over their years of seeking and knowing God. The two youngest generations—the Mosaics and the Busters—are most likely to resonate with that style of interaction. Facilitating those opportunities would be valuable for both parties.

Generally genial and relational, widowed people want social opportunities without pressure to participate. They want to be known and cared for but not relied upon for production. Because most widowed people are elderly women, one of the consistent needs expressed is for peers in the faith to keep an eye on their health-care and housing situations. They expect their church to demonstrate an interest in their welfare and to lend a hand in tying loose ends together when they need assistance.

WHAT DIVORCED ADULTS NEED

Life is a wild seesaw ride for many divorced adults. Divorced singles typically feel physically fatigued, emotionally drained, financially strapped and spiritually confused. They generally wallow in uncertainty about getting remarried and maintaining viable relationships with their children (if they have any) from their former marriage. These are people who are stressed and need maximum space and understanding. They will be irritating sometimes because they want control, but that is merely a product of their insecurity, distrust and hectic lives.

Don't expect most divorced adults to get really excited about church involvement. There is a great level of fear of rejection and abandonment—again—by other Christians due to their divorce. Consequently, their spirituality is often a very meaningful but private affair. Persuading them to engage in corporate spiritual life will take time, sensitivity and perceived benefits. They have no time to waste and no energy to spare—make it great or get out of their way.

Many divorced people retain a level of anger with God—*How could He let this happen to me?*—that does not subside for years, if ever. When it comes to their faith, they want to make it real and central to their lives but only if they can see the benefit and also work it around all the imperatives in their pressure-packed lives. Chances are good that they don't really understand worship, they have only a passing knowledge of the Bible, they have no time for community-service efforts, and they feel they cannot afford to return God's resources as a good steward would. In other words, they will view their circumstances as a viable excuse for not engaging with God in as deep a way as they need to. Coaching them into a slowly growing commitment is your best bet.

ARE THEY WORTH IT?

If you are developing a ministry to single adults through your church, you might consider the value of a "stealth singles ministry," that is, a ministry that focuses on helping single adults but outside the boundaries of the typical "singles ghetto." More and more we are hearing from singles that they do not want to live outside the mainstream of the congregation simply because they are not married. They want to be completely bonded to the heartbeat of the church and get their singles fix in some other way. Ministries that integrate singles provide that personalized touch through events designed to aid singles and through developed relational networks that meet their unique needs.

Now that you know many of the complexities of singles and just how challenging such a ministry might be, are you asking whether ministry to single adults is worth the effort? (If you're not, I suspect you're not paying attention!) In arriving at an answer, consider these two thoughts.

SINGLES DO NOT WANT TO LIVE OUTSIDE THE MAINSTREAM OF THE CONGREGATION SIMPLY BECAUSE THEY ARE NOT MARRIED.

First, God loves all of His people. He does not discriminate on the basis of their marital status. (In fact, some would make the argument that Paul's admonition to stay single, if possible, suggests that God recognizes the benefits of remaining single.) Singles are precious to Him. He dearly loves them and, therefore, so should we.

Second, if the Bible is meant to direct and shape our thoughts about ministry, then keep in mind that more than a few of the greatest leaders and examples in Scripture were single. These patrons of our faith demonstrate the dramatic impact an unmarried person can have upon the world. From Ruth and Mary to John the Baptist and Paul—and even Jesus—the Bible underscores the significant contributions of singles. It is our privilege to know and love and serve them. It is my prayer that through this book you are now blessed with additional knowledge that will make that task easier and more fulfilling.

RESEARCH METHODOLOGY

This book is based on data derived from eight nationwide surveys among adults, conducted by the Barna Research Group, Ltd., of Ventura, California. In each survey, a random sample of adults was drawn from the 48 continental states and a survey questionnaire was administered to individuals. These telephone surveys were conducted from the Barna Research field facility in Ventura. The timing and related statistics pertaining to those surveys are shown in table A.1.

TABLE A.1

OmniPoll™	Date Conducted	Sample Size Total	Singles
OP 1-00	January 2000	1002	469
OP S-00	April 2000	1003	458
OP 2-00	July 2000	1008	446
OP F-00	November 2000	1017	479
OP 1-01	January 2001	1005	504
OP S-01	April 2001	1003	491
OP 2-01	August 2001	1001	496
OP F-01	November 2001	1010	474

The surveys were conducted through the use of the random-digit-dial (RDD) sampling technique. In this method, we derive a representative nationwide sample of telephone numbers that have been randomly generated. We then call the household and screen respondents to determine whether or not a qualified person lives in the home. If there is, we attempt to conduct the interview with the individual. While we are not able to connect with every eligible adult whose home we call, our response rates in qualified households still exceed industry norms. In these surveys, the response rates averaged 71 percent in the qualified households. The average survey lasted anywhere from 16 to 21 minutes per respondent. The maximum amount of sampling error associated with the aggregate survey is plus or minus 3 percentage points at the 95 percent confidence level. The maximum sampling error associated with the singles subgroups is approximately plus or minus 5 percentage points.

ABOUT THE BARNA RESEARCH GROUP, LTD.

The Barna Research Group (BRG) was initiated in 1984 by George and Nancy Barna to serve the information needs of the Church. BRG's vision is "to provide Christian ministries with current, accurate and reliable information, in bite-sized pieces, at reasonable cost, to help them to be more strategic in their decision making." The company has been honored to serve thousands of ministries since its inception.

Barna Research helps ministries by

- offering a wealth of free, current information online, through the BRG website (http://www.barna.org) and the biweekly publication of its latest findings (*The Barna Update*);
- conducting primary research related to specific information, development and marketing needs of an organization;

- providing resources—books, reports, videos, audiocassettes and newsletters—that describe BRG's research and how the findings apply to ministry;
- conducting intensive classes and seminars for church leaders, which reveal insights from primary research conducted for the seminar;
- presenting information in conferences, seminars and other meetings;
- providing research-based consultation related to articulated ministry needs.

BRG uses both quantitative and qualitative research methods to generate relevant and reliable information that reveals insights to enhance ministry efforts.

Among the types of research commonly conducted by BRG are

- attitudinal and behavioral surveys of congregations;
- lifestyle, value, behavior and belief profiles of communities;
- profiles of the attitudes, expectations, giving habits and needs of donors;
- evaluations of new products (i.e., perceived value, pricing, marketing and so on);
- name recognition and ministry image studies;
- employee perception studies;
- efficiency and effectiveness studies;
- product-use studies;
- customer service and customer satisfaction;
- segmentation studies to identify tapped and untapped potential;
- media use surveys.

If you would like to know more about Barna Research, please explore our website. If you are interested in conducting primary research to solve some of your ministry and marketing challenges, call us at 1-800-55-BARNA. For further information, visit the Barna Research Group, Ltd., website at http://www.barna.org.

A P P E N D I X   C

TAKING ADVANTAGE OF BARNA RESEARCH

Because our commitment is to help the Church live up to its God-given calling, we try to support ministries with strategic information. While the books and reports we develop contain much of this data and related interpretation, we have also created a website geared to arming ministers—lay and professional—with the strategic intelligence they need to make great decisions in ministry. Here are some suggestions on using our services.

1. **Visit our website: http://www.barna.org.** Explore the various pages on the site to discover what we have to offer. Although you may not need it all today, it might be useful in the future.
2. **Subscribe to our free e-publication, *The Barna Update*, which is available only through the website.** Every two weeks or so, George Barna releases a new report based upon the most recent

information from Barna Research surveys. Sign up and you will automatically receive a very brief e-mail on the day the study is released, which will inform you of the report topic and two or three key findings. If the topic interests you, click on the link provided with the e-mail (or go to our website) to read the entire release. We have included a "click and send" function enabling you to send the report to others whom you feel would benefit from it. (By the way, if you subscribe, we will not give out your e-mail address or spam you!)

3. **Use the data archives.** We have put hundreds of factoids and data morsels into 40 different categories that you can access. Need facts for a sermon? Ideas on how to make a Scripture passage seem more relevant? Want to understand what people are thinking and doing in relation to a specific topic? Interested in understanding more about different segments of the population? Use this 24/7 library of faith facts whenever you're seeking a particular insight.

4. **Acquire related resources.** If you are interested in additional information on specific topics, check out the reports, books, diagnostics, videos, audiocassettes and other resources based on our research that is available to you. Some of these resources can be obtained only through our website.

5. **Read Barna's reviews of other valuable ministry resources.** Several thousand new Christian books and related resources are produced every year. This section of the website provides reviews of recent resources to help you identify which ones might be most valuable to your own ministry and spiritual development.

We are constantly updating and expanding our website contents. We pray that you use it and profit from it. Let us know what else you want on the site. It's there for you.

http://www.barna.org

ENDNOTES

Chapter 1

1. U.S. Bureau of the Census, *Statistical Abstract of the United States, 2001* (Washington, DC), table 1327; Barna Research Group, 2000-2001 survey data.
2. Ibid., table 49.
3. George Barna, "Born-Again Adults Less Likely to Cohabit, Just As Likely to Divorce," *Barna Research Online Home Page,* August 6, 2001. http://www.barna.org/cgi-bin/PagePressRelease.asp?PressReleaseD=95&Reference=B (accessed 2001).
4. Those 11 nations are Bangladesh, Brazil, China, Germany, India, Indonesia, Japan, Mexico, Nigeria, Pakistan and Russia.
5. U.S. Bureau of the Census, *Statistical Abstract of the United States, 2001* (Washington, DC), table 57.
6. National Center for Health Statistics, *Vital Statistics of the United States, 2001* (Washington, DC), p. 42.
7. Ibid.
8. Centers for Disease Control and Prevention, *Centers for Disease Control and Prevention Home Page,* May 24, 2001. http://www.cdc.gov.
9. U.S. Bureau of the Census, "Table A1: Marital Status of People 15 Years and Over, by Age, Sex, Personal Earnings, Race and Hispanic Origin/March 2000," *Census Bureau Home Page,* released June 29, 2001. http://www.census.gov (accessed June 29, 2001).
10. Ibid.
11. The Centers for Disease Control and Prevention issued the report "First Marriage Dissolution, Divorce and Remarriage in the United States" in May 2001. The report indicated that one-fifth of marriages result in divorce within 5 years, one-third within 10 years and 43 percent within 15 years.

12. Barna Research Group, 2000-2001 survey data, N=7,996 (N=sample size).

13. This perspective is perhaps best explained in Barbara Dafoe Whitehead's *The Divorce Culture* (New York: Alfred Knopf, 1997).

14. U.S. Bureau of the Census, *Statistical Abstract of the United States, 2000* (Washington, DC), table 64.

15. U.S. Bureau of the Census, "Table A1: Marital Status of People 15 Years and Over, by Age, Sex, Personal Earnings, Race and Hispanic Origin/March 2000," *Census Bureau Home Page,* released June 29, 2001. http://www.census.gov.

16. U.S. Bureau of the Census, *Statistical Abstract of the United States, 2000* (Washington, DC), table 55.

17. Ibid., table 1213.

18. Ibid., tables 738-741.

19. Ibid.

Chapter 2

1. For a deeper discussion of the spiritual condition of America, examine the research described in my book *Growing True Disciples* (Colorado Springs, CO: WaterBrook, 2001).

2. These conclusions are drawn from studies we have been conducting among teenagers whose parents divorce and/or whose closest friends' parents divorce, the results of which studies show young people's perspectives shift from being comfortable with the Christian faith to being uncomfortable with all faith groups.

3. Let me point out that when I use the term "born-again" to describe a person, it is *not* based upon their self-identification as such. Barna Research uses a two-question approach to determine the likelihood of a person being born-again. Our data reveal that only a moderate correlation exists between people calling themselves born-again Christians and actually having a relationship with Christ based upon confession of sins and acceptance of His grace. See chapter 7 for further details.

Chapter 3

1. This data is from a national survey by the Barna Research Group, July 2001. The study randomly surveyed 1,002 adults, including 496 single adults.

2. California Survey Research, *USA Today* (February 9, 1999), p. D-1.

3. Bureau of Labor Statistics, "Consumer Expenditure Survey" *Bureau of Labor Statistics Home Page,* 1999. http://www.bls.gov.

4. Pamela Paul, "Coming Soon," *American Demographics* (August 2001), p. 30.

5. U.S. Bureau of the Census, *Statistical Abstract of the United States, 2000* (Washington, DC), tables 418-427.

6. Ibid., tables 55, 96, 97.

7. Centers for Disease Control, *Health, United States, 2001* (Washington, DC), table 16, p. 148.

8. U.S. Bureau of the Census, *Statistical Abstract of the United States, 2000* (Washington, DC), tables 103, 113.

9. Ibid., table 78.

10. *Washington Watch* (December 2000), p. 8.
11. U.S. Bureau of the Census, *Statistical Abstract of the United States, 2000* (Washington, DC), tables 738, 741.
12. Ibid., table 1213.
13. Ibid., tables 738, 741.
14. Peter Hart Research, *Advertising Age* (August 24, 1998), p. 35.
15. Bureau of Labor Statistics, "Consumer Expenditure Survey" *Bureau of Labor Statistics Home Page,* 1999. http://www.bls.gov.

Chapter 4

1. A national survey by the Barna Research Group, January 2000 and November 2001. The study randomly surveyed single adults.
2. Jennifer Day and Avalaura Gaither, *Current Population Report: Voting and Registration in the Election of November 1998,* a special report prepared at the request of the U.S. Bureau of the Census (Washington, DC: U.S. Census Bureau, August 2000), table C.
3. A more extensive discussion of this trend is included in my book *Real Teens* (Ventura, CA: Regal Books, 2001), which notes the misleading nature of the current high level of church involvement among teenagers and what we might expect in the future.
4. This study was conducted in September 1998 and reported in *Rolling Stone* (November 12, 1998), pp. 79-80.
5. A national survey by the Pew Research Center, September 2000.
6. A national survey by the Barna Research Group, May 2001. The study randomly surveyed 1,003 adults.
7. U.S. Bureau of the Census, *Statistical Abstract of the United States, 2000* (Washington, DC), table 57.
8. This data from the U.S. Bureau of the Census was reported in *Pastor's Weekly Briefing* (May 12, 2000), p. 2.
9. These facts were drawn from several sources, including the U.S. Bureau of the Census data reported in *AFA Journal* (September 1998), p. 9; Professor Susan Brown of Bowling Green State University, reported in *SAM Journal* (September-October 1998), p. 28; and Professor Larry Bumpass of the University of Wisconsin, cited in *Newsweek* (November 2, 1998), p. 60.
10. University of Michigan's Survey Research Center, *Research Alert Yearbook 2000* (New York: EPM Communications, 2000), p. 81.
11. Ibid.
12. Ibid.
13. The CDC and Guttmacher statistics were reported in *Pastor's Weekly Briefing* (January 16, 1998), p. 2.
14. A nationwide telephone survey by the Pew Research Center, October 2000.
15. NORC, *General Social Survey of 1998* (University of Chicago), n.p.
16. *AFA Journal* (September 1998), p. 9.
17. For more details on this study, consult the National Marriage Project research conducted by Rutgers University, New Jersey. This survey involved interviews with 1,003 single adults in the 20- to 29-year-old age group.
18. A nationwide telephone survey by the Pew Research Center, March 2001.

19. Ibid.
20. A national survey by the Barna Research Group, May 2001. The study randomly surveyed 1,003 adults.
21. Ibid.
22. Ibid.
23. Ibid.

Chapter 5

1. National telephone interviews by the Barna Research Group, January 2000-July 2001. The study randomly interviewed 2,847 single adults.
2. Ibid.
3. A more extensive discussion of the integration of the pillars of faith into vital ministry is contained in my book *The Habits of Highly Effective Churches* (Ventura, CA: Regal Books, 1999). We discovered that the churches where people's lives are being transformed to greater Christlikeness have nine key habits, which focus on the six pillars, plus three habits that facilitate the development of mature faith in those areas.
4. The discussion here centers on the six pillars of faith but analyzes reactions to eight aspects of faith pursuit. The reason for the discrepancy in the number of elements discussed is that both the discipleship and fellowship functions were broken into two elements in order to convey their substance more completely.
5. A nationwide telephone survey by the Barna Research Group, November 2000. The study randomly interviewed 1,002 adults, including 479 single adults.
6. A nationwide telephone survey by the Barna Research Group, January 2000. The study randomly surveyed 1,004 adults, including 469 single adults.
7. Ibid.

Chapter 6

1. A nationwide telephone survey by the Barna Research Group, January 2001. The study randomly surveyed 1,003 adults, including 504 single adults.
2. Figures from an analysis of eight national quarterly tracking studies of church attendance by the Barna Research Group, January 2000-November 2001. The study involved more than 8,000 adults, including 3,817 single adults.
3. A national survey by the Barna Research Group, October-November 2001. The study randomly interviewed 1,001 adults, including 496 single adults.
4. Nationwide telephone surveys by the Barna Research Group, January 2000-July 2001. The study randomly surveyed 3,148 married adults and 2,847 single adults.
5. Ibid.
6. A nationwide telephone survey by the Barna Research Group, October-November 2001. The study randomly interviewed 1,001 adults, including 496 single adults.
7. All data on giving is based on the annual tracking study of national giving patterns by the Barna Research Group, January 2000. The study randomly surveyed 1,002 adults, including 504 single adults.

8. Nationwide telephone surveys by the Barna Research Group, January 2000-July 2001. The study randomly interviewed 3,148 married adults and 2,847 single adults.

Chapter 7

1. This study is based on a nationally representative random sample of 8,049 adults. Those included interviews with 3,817 singles. Of those, 2,237 had never been married, 949 were currently divorced, and 631 were widowed.

2. It is important to keep in mind that only God knows the true heart of a person, and thus only He knows if a person is truly born-again. Our research is not an attempt to judge people but to estimate what seems to be happening in regard to salvation and personal relationships with Jesus. I use the term "born-again Christian" to describe those who say they have made a personal commitment to Jesus, which remains important to them, and who expect to inhabit heaven because they have acknowledged their sins, asked for God's forgiveness and rely upon Christ as their Savior. These descriptions help differentiate true born-again Christians from the multitudes who call themselves Christian but have no such basis for their faith and hope for eternity.

Chapter 8

1. For a deeper discussion of this process, see my book *Turning Vision into Action* (Ventura, CA: Regal Books, 1994), which will help you understand, identify, articulate and pursue God's vision for your life.

Chapter 9

1. One of the diagnostic tools we have developed is the Personal Spiritual Inventory, a simple and quick way of determining where a person stands in regard to the six pillars of faith—worship, evangelism, personal spiritual development, resource stewardship, community service and fellowship. For more information about this self-administered inventory, consult the Barna Research Group website at http://www.barna.org.